RATS, BATS, AND XENARTHRANS

THE BRITANNICA GUIDE TO PREDATORS AND PREY

RATS, BATS, AND XENARTHRANS

EDITED BY JOHN P. RAFFERTY, ASSOCIATE EDITOR, EARTH AND LIFE SCIENCES

Britannica®
Educational Publishing

IN ASSOCIATION WITH

ROSEN
EDUCATIONAL SERVICES

Published in 2011 by Britannica Educational Publishing
(a trademark of Encyclopædia Britannica, Inc.)
in association with Rosen Educational Services, LLC
29 East 21st Street, New York, NY 10010.

Distributed exclusively by Rosen Educational Services.
For a listing of additional Britannica Educational Publishing titles, call toll free (800) 237-9932.

First Edition

Britannica Educational Publishing
Michael I. Levy: Executive Editor
J.E. Luebering: Senior Manager
Marilyn L. Barton: Senior Coordinator, Production Control
Steven Bosco: Director, Editorial Technologies
Lisa S. Braucher: Senior Producer and Data Editor
Yvette Charboneau: Senior Copy Editor
Kathy Nakamura: Manager, Media Acquisition
John P. Rafferty: Associate Editor, Earth and Life Sciences

Rosen Educational Services
Hope Lourie Killcoyne: Senior Editor and Project Manager
Nelson Sá: Art Director
Cindy Reiman: Photography Manager
Matthew Cauli: Designer, Cover Design
Introduction by Charles Doersch

Library of Congress Cataloging-in-Publication Data

Rats, bats, and xenarthrans / edited by John P. Rafferty. — 1st ed.
    p. cm. — (The Britannica guide to predators and prey)
"In association with Britannica Educational Publishing, Rosen Educational Services."
Includes bibliographical references and index.
ISBN 978-1-61530-332-8 (library binding)
1. Rats—Juvenile literature. 2. Bats—Juvenile literature. 3. Xenarthra—Juvenile literature.
I. Rafferty, John P.
QL737.R666R39 2011
599.35—dc22

                                                                    2010029000

Manufactured in the United States of America

On the cover: Three-toed sloths, such as this young one in southern Costa Rica's Osa Peninsula, are a kind of xenarthran, a group of mammals the origins of which can be traced back some 65 million years. Along with sloths, anteaters and armadillos are also in the xenarthra group. *Roy Toft/National Geographic Image Collection/Getty Images*

On page xviii: A young capybara (*Hydrochoerus hydrochaeris*). The capybara is the world's largest rodent; South American capybaras may be 1.25 metres (over 4 feet) long and weigh 66 kg (145 pounds) or more. *Shutterstock.com*

On pages 1, 8, 44, 80, 119, 153, 202, 221, 227, 231: Juvenile ground squirrels (genus *Spermophilus*) in the Rio Grande Valley, TX. Ground squirrels have a single litter of four to nine young a year. *Jeremy Woodhouse/Photodisc/Getty Images*

CONTENTS

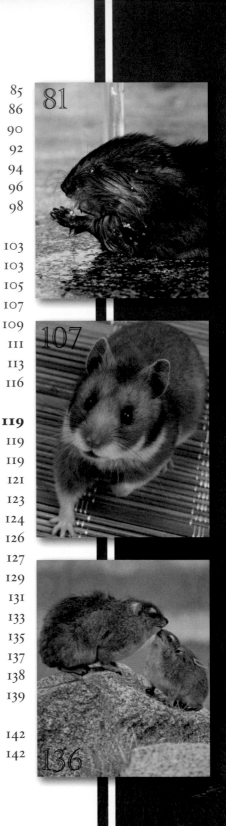

81

107

136

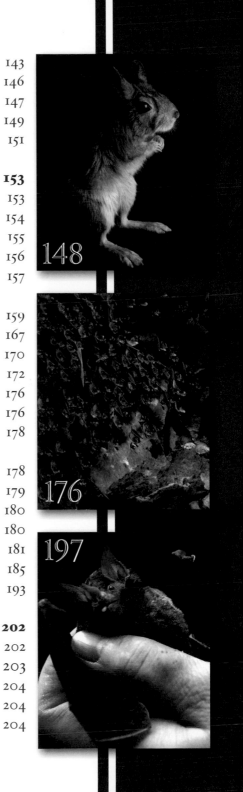

148

176

197

INTRODUCTION

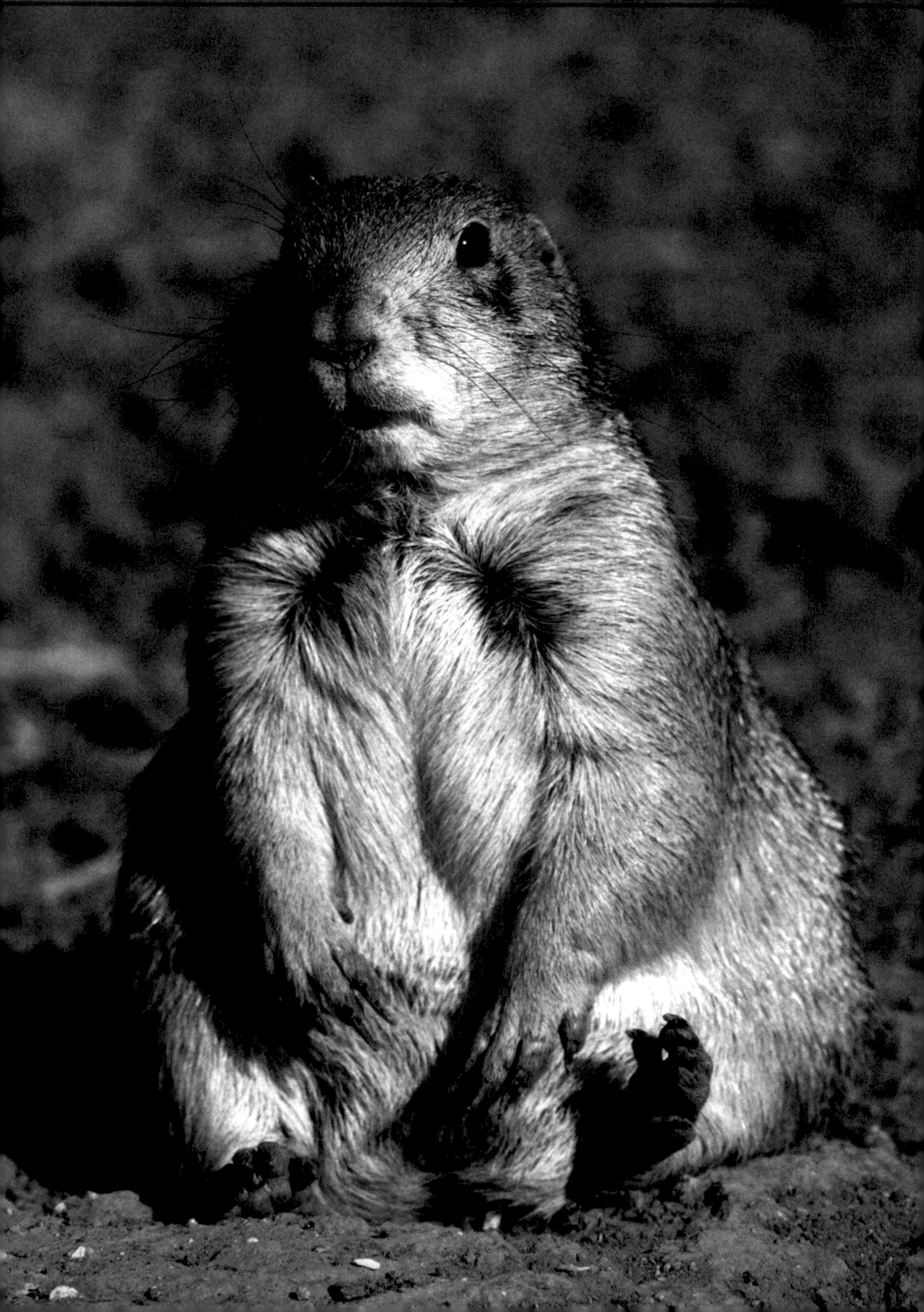

Rodents and bats are familiar to us, and for good reason: two-thirds of all mammal species on the planet are either one or the other. When you look closely at the enormous diversity of shapes and sizes that these two orders of mammals have developed, and consider the range of habitats they can survive in, it becomes clear that their ubiquity on the planet is the result of the adaptability and resiliency inherent in their genetic makeup. It is frankly incredible.

On the other hand, xenarthrans—armadillos, sloths, and anteaters—are much less diverse and widespread. They represent only 29 of the 4,660 mammal species we know of. For whatever reasons, these mammals are more narrowly specialized, less diverse, more "traditional," and less adaptive; they are consequently rare, and several are in danger of extinction (the outstanding exception being the plucky nine-banded armadillo, whose range now stretches from Argentina to the southern United States).

This book will examine some of what we know so far about the great range of forms and behaviours of three fascinating and very different groups of animals: rodents, bats, and xenarthrans.

The mammalian order with the greatest number of species is *Rodentia*. Fully 44 percent of all mammal species are some variety of rodent—that's an astounding 2,055 species. Rodents are native to every land area on earth except Antarctica, New Zealand, and some oceanic islands (though they have subsequently reached just about everywhere by hitching rides with humans). All rodents have

A black-tailed prairie dog (Cynomys ludovicianus) *sits for a spell. Prairie dogs are the most sociable members of the squirrel family. At the approach of predators, prairie dogs warn other members of their group with a chirp-like bark.* Jeff Foott/Discovery Channel Images/Getty Images

certain features in common. Their well-known, chisel-like incisor teeth and their sharp claws are great for digging or climbing, but other features can vary widely. Take size, for instance. Delany's swamp mouse in Africa—one of the smallest rodents—measures only 6 cm (about 2 inches) long. The capybara of Central and South America, on the other hand, is the largest rodent living today, growing up to 60 cm (2 feet) tall at the shoulder, and more than 1.35 metres (over 4 feet) long.

Rodents are among the most adaptable mammals on Earth. They can be nocturnal, diurnal, or active during both day and night. Some climb, some swim, some burrow, some soar, some jump. Some create huge colonies (such as prairie dogs) that can cover tens of thousands of square acres, whereas others live strictly alone. One group, the beavers, can fell large trees, construct elaborate dams across creeks, and dig canals between water sources. Although some rodents are herbivores, most are opportunistic generalists, eating whatever is convenient at the time. Some species, however, are specialized predators, not only of arthropods (grasshoppers, spiders, ants, etc.), but also of vertebrates (such as bird nestlings, lizards, snakes, etc.). Most rodents eat their food wherever they find it, whereas others, such as certain species of squirrels, gather up food and store it in large piles underground, or under leaves, or in basements or attics. Many rodents need water, but others, such as the kangaroo rat at Great Sand Dunes National Park in Colorado, are very efficient at obtaining the water needed from the food it eats, and so are at home in the driest desert.

All this is simply to say, that when we compare the lives of different species of rodents, *variety* is what we see.

Certainly two of the most successful and adaptable rodent families are those of mice and rats. It appears that these two groups are especially adept at adapting to human-made environments. Since the dawn of towns and cities, wherever humans settled, rats and mice moved in. Although rodents could frequently be used as a food source for humans, urban living has inadvertently provided reliable food and shelter opportunities for rodents, as well. The animals' ability to quickly reproduce coupled with their tenacity in the face of obstacles forced humans to view them as serious pests. Rodents are capable of ruining crops before harvest, spoiling stored foodstuffs after harvest, gnawing through containers, infesting structures, digging under fences, and spreading disease.

Mice and rats often suffer from a disconnect between their common names and taxonomic placement. Not every species commonly called "rats" or "mice" are true rats or mice. The kangaroo rat, for example, is not a rat, and the birch mouse is not a true mouse—but they *are* rodents.

However, when is a mouse *not* a mouse, and *not* even a rodent? When it's a bat, of course. Long ago, before modern science, Europeans considered bats as mice that could fly. In fact, the name for "bat" in many languages has the name "mouse" in it. Whether it's the "fluttering mouse" of Germany, Scandinavia, and Russia, or the "blind mouse" of Spanish-speaking countries, languages often connect bats to mice. But bats, of course, are not rodents; they belong to an ancient order of animals called *Chiroptera* (which means "hand wings" in Greek) and are the only mammals that can fly. "Hand wings" is an apt description for them; the skeletons of bats show "fingers" that have elongated to become the bones of their wings, with soft leathery skin stretched between.

As a group, bats, like rodents, occur widely across the planet. Bats are found from Alaska to the tropics and all around the world. The only places they do not occur are in the polar regions and some very remote islands.

Considering the immense variety of bats, it is clear that they are almost as successful as rodents in adapting to a diversity of habitats, climates, and food sources. There are more than a thousand species of bats, and they comprise nearly a quarter of all mammal species.

Like rodents, bats come in all sizes, and are generally dividable among two suborders: *Megachiroptera* (megabats) and *Microchiroptera* (microbats).

Megabats have fox-like faces and large eyes. They live only in the tropics, generally eat fruit, roost in trees, and grow to larger sizes; some have wingspans up to 1.5 metres (5 feet).

The bodies of microbats, on the other hand, approximate the size of mice or rats. However, some, such as the bumblebee bat, are no bigger than a large moth, with a wingspan of just 60 cm (6 inches) and a body weighing less than a dime. Microbats have small eyes and use echolocation to find food and avoid bumping into objects (and each other) in the night.

Most microbats are insectivores, and thus benefit humans by keeping the populations of certain insects in check. Consider the Mexican free-tailed bat, for example. It is only one of many chiropterans in Texas, but this species alone consumes an estimated 10,000 tons of insects every year. Throughout the world, bats flitter through the night sky gobbling up moths, mosquitoes, flies, midges, and other bugs. In fact, the erratic, jerky path of a bat's flight results from its attempts to catch flying insects. When there is nothing to catch, bats fly straight and smoothly. Of course, not all bat species eat insects. Some feed off the nectar and pollen of flowers, whereas others prey on fish, birds, and other small animals. Many bats are frugivorous (fruit-eating), and some—just three species— live off blood (true vampire bats).

The great variety of habitats bats thrive in is indicative of their wide tolerance for different roost types. The challenges posed by the roosts may affect how different species of bats mate with one another and raise their young. Bats do tend to prefer roosting in colonies and groups, but often the females and their young have separate areas; the females and young of some species roost away from the males.

As detailed in this book, the evolutionary adaptations of bats' bodies is marvellous and strange; it is difficult to imagine any group of mammals that has changed so much over time.

Then again, "marvelous and strange" would also be a fitting description for the xenarthrans—an ancient lineage of mammals comprised of armadillos, sloths, and anteaters. However, unlike the worldwide adaptability presence of rodents and bats, xenarthrans live only in Latin America—all of them, that is, except the nine-banded armadillo, whose range reaches from South America up into the southern United States.

Armadillos are unusual in many ways. Covered from head to tail in bony plates, they range in size from the 16-cm (6-inch) pink fairy armadillo to the 1.8-metre (6-foot) giant anteater.

Armadillos' reproduction is also unusual. For example, nine-banded armadillos bear young as sets of identical quadruplets that develop in the uterus from a single fertilized egg. Even more astonishing, it can be months after mating before the egg begins to develop. After mating occurs, females can travel long distances to new territories before the four-month gestation period begins. This adaptation has undoubtedly contributed to the species' successful range expansion.

Like all xenarthrans, armadillos possess slow metabolisms; they burn calories at less than half the rate of other similarly sized mammals. A slow metabolism leads to a lower body temperature, which in turn means that these animals are more particularly vulnerable to cold. Thus a sudden change in the weather—such as a cold snap—could kill an individual very quickly.

Armadillos are fairly flexible in their food choices, eating a variety of plant matter, worms, insects, and small animals. In this gastronomic eclecticism, they differ from their more "fussy" fellow xenarthrans—the sloths, who eat only leaves, and anteaters, who prefer insects.

Excellent diggers, armadillos excavate deep, long burrows underground in which they sleep away the daylight hours, emerging at night to forage for food. Their digging habits can get them in trouble with people, however, causing property damage or stepping hazards for livestock. Thus, they are treated as pests in many places. With only twenty living species, armadillos are nonetheless the most numerous of the xenarthrans—and most are endangered. By comparison, there are only five species of sloths and four species of anteaters.

Sloths, famously slow in their movements, are shaggy tree-dwelling mammals that are divided into two families: two-toed sloths and three-toed sloths. With long arms and short legs, these appendages are designed for suspending the body rather than supporting it. Sloths are content hanging beneath branches by their hooked toes for hours and hours, sunning, sleeping, and eating leaves. In the event they fall to the ground, sloths are nearly helpless: they cannot stand up, they cannot run away from predators, and they do not defend themselves well. In addition, they have poor sight and bad hearing. How do they survive? By camouflage: algae grow in their hair and give them a gray-green colour. Sloths are difficult to see during the day, live high up in the forest canopy, and move so slowly during the night that other animals (including humans) often do not notice them. Because sloths are very difficult to keep in captivity, scientists do not have a full understanding of their life cycle.

Anteaters differ from armadillos and sloths in many ways. They have no teeth, their muzzle is tubular with a tiny opening, and they have an extensible sticky tongue. In addition, anteaters subsist almost entirely on ants, termites, and other social insects. Like their sloth cousins, anteaters are covered in thick fur, and like the armadillos, they can dig into termite mounds with strong claws. Anteaters range in size from the giant anteater, which can grow to a length of 1.8 metres (6 feet), down to the silky anteater, which rarely exceeds 44 cm (17 inches). Anteaters are found from tropical grasslands to the floors and canopies of tropical forests.

This book provides a substantial cross-section of the range of mammalian diversity. Readers will be taken deep into the surprising world of rodents, chiropterans, and xenarthrans. Along the way, readers will be exposed to the discoveries scientists have made in understanding who these creatures are, how they live, and the value of their incredible and varied adaptations.

CHAPTER 1

RODENTS

There are more than 2,050 living species of rodents (order Rodentia)—mammals characterized by upper and lower pairs of ever-growing rootless incisor teeth. Rodents are the largest group of mammals, constituting almost half the class Mammalia's approximately 4,660 species. They are indigenous to every land area except Antarctica, New Zealand, and a few Arctic and other oceanic islands, although some species have been introduced even to those places through their association with humans. This huge order of animals encompasses 27 separate families, including not only the "true" rats and mice (family Muridae) but also such diverse groups as porcupines, beavers, squirrels, marmots, pocket gophers, and chinchillas.

GENERAL FEATURES

All rodents possess constantly growing rootless incisors that have a hard enamel layer on the front of each tooth and softer dentine behind. The differential wear from gnawing creates perpetually sharp chisel edges. Rodents' absence of other incisors and canine teeth results in a gap, or diastema, between incisors and cheekteeth, which number from 22 (5 on each side of the upper and lower jaws) to 4, may be rooted or rootless and ever-growing, and may be low- or high-crowned. The nature of the jaw articulation ensures that incisors do not meet when food is chewed and that upper and lower cheekteeth (premolars and molars) do not make contact while the animal gnaws. Powerful and intricately divided masseter muscles,

attached to jaw and skull in different arrangements, provide most of the power for chewing and gnawing.

The range in body size between the mouse (18 grams
[0.64 ounce], body 12 cm [4.7 inches] long) and the marmot (3,000 grams [6.6 pounds], body 50 cm [19.7 inches]
long) spans the *majority* of living rodents, but the extremes
are remarkable. One of the smallest is Delany's swamp
mouse (*Delanymys brooksi*), associated with bamboo in
the marshes and mountain forests in Africa. It weighs 5
to 7 grams (0.18 to 0.25 ounce), and the body is 5 to 6 cm
(2 to 2.4 inches) long. The largest rodent is the capybara
(*Hydrochoerus hydrochaeris*) of Central and South America,
which weighs 35 to 66 kg (77 to 146 pounds) and stands
50 to 60 cm (20 to 24 inches) at the shoulder, with a body
100 to 135 cm (39.4 to 53.2 inches) long. Some extinct species were even larger, attaining the size of a black bear
or small rhinoceros. The largest rodent ever recorded,
Josephoartigasia monesi, lived some two to four million years
ago, during the Pleistocene and Pliocene epochs. By some
estimates it grew to a length of about 3 metres (10 feet)
and weighed nearly 1,000 kg (about 2,200 pounds).

IMPORTANCE TO HUMANS

Rodents have lived on the planet for at least 56 million
years and modern humans for less than one million, but
the consequences of their interactions during that short
overlap of evolutionary time have been profound. For
rodents, early humans were just another predator to avoid,
but with *Homo sapiens'* transition from nomadic hunting
and gathering to sedentary agricultural practices, humans
became a reliable source of shelter and food for those species having the innate genetic and behavioral abilities to
adapt to man-made habitats. The impact of these species upon human populations ranges from inconvenient

to deadly. Crops are damaged before harvest; stored food is contaminated by rodent waste; water-impounding structures leak from burrowing; and objects are damaged by gnawing. Certain species are reservoirs for diseases, including plague, murine typhus, scrub typhus, tularemia, rat-bite fever, Rocky Mountain spotted fever, and Lassa fever. Only a few species are serious pests or vectors of disease, but it is these rodents that are most closely associated with people.

Various other rodents are beneficial, providing a source of food through hunting and husbandry, apparel derived from their fur, test animals for biomedical and genetic research (especially mice and rats), pleasure as household pets, and insight on mammalian biology and evolutionary history.

NATURAL HISTORY

Rodents may be diurnal, nocturnal, or sometimes active part of the day and night. Although some species are herbivorous, the diets of most include both vegetable and animal matter. When in search of meat, there are what might be called opportunistic generalists, as well as others that are specialized predators—not only of arthropods but sometimes of vertebrates. Food is either eaten where gathered or carried to burrows and stored (the latter option being favored by the pocket mouse, African pouched rat, and hamster). Species living in arid habitats and on oceanic islands are able to obtain their water requirements from their food. A wide variety of shelters are used or constructed, ranging from tree holes, rock crevices, or simple burrows, to hidden nests on the forest floor, leaf and stick structures in tree crowns, mounds of cut vegetation built in aquatic environments, or complex networks of tunnels and galleries. Rodents may be active all year or enter periods of dormancy or deep hibernation. Breeding time and frequency, length of gestation, and litter size vary widely, but two of the most prolific species are both associated with humans. The brown rat (*Rattus norvegicus*) can give birth to litters of up to 22 offspring, and the house mouse (*Mus musculus*) can produce up to 14 litters annually, the average birth resulting in 5 to 6 offspring, with as many as 12 per birth occasionally occurring, as well. Rodent population size may remain stable or fluctuate, and some species, most notably lemmings, migrate when groups become excessively large.

MURIDAE

Muridae is the largest extant rodent family—indeed the largest of all mammalian families—encompassing more than 1,383 species of the "true" mice and rats. Two-thirds of all rodent species and genera belong to family Muridae. The members of this family are often collectively called murids, or muroid rodents.

The 300 genera of muroid rodents are classified within 18 subfamilies, but more than 200 of them (and nearly 1,000 species) belong to only two subfamilies—Sigmodontinae (New World rats and mice) and Murinae (Old World rats and mice). Two other subfamilies (Arvicolinae and Gerbillinae) include approximately 250 additional species, with the remaining 14 subfamilies accommodating various other genera, some of which consist of a single species.

Not all specialists agree on the number of subfamilies or that all of these should be included within Muridae. For instance, some assemblages, such as blind mole rats and bamboo rats, are very distinctive and have been treated in the past as separate families. The Malabar spiny tree mouse was originally described as a kind of dormouse (*Myoxidae*), but was reclassified as a murid similar to blind tree mice. Many subfamilies, including hamsters, were formerly considered as part of a family separate from Muridae, but these groups are now most often viewed as muroid subfamilies. Inclusion of these subfamilies emphasizes their closer evolutionary relationships to one another than to any other group of rodents, but such

4

affinity could also be expressed by recognizing each as a separate family and then bringing them together within a larger category, the superfamily Muroidea. This would be satisfactory if each group could be clearly demonstrated to have a common ancestor (i.e., to be monophyletic). Some groups are known to be monophyletic (hamsters, voles, African pouched rats, gerbils, Old World rats and mice, African spiny mice, platacanthomyines, zokors, blind mole rats, and bamboo rats). Other groups, however, cannot be classified with certainty and may or may not be a hodgepodge of unrelated genera and species (New World rats and mice, dendromurines, and Malagasy rats and mice). Also unresolved are the affinities of subfamilies containing only one genus (mouselike hamsters, the maned rat).

Pending better resolution of the relationships between these problem groups, some specialists prefer to retain them as subfamilies within Muridae, but others still separate them as families under the umbrella of Muroidea. Fossil evidence may support the single-family arrangement because clearly diagnosable groups of living species, such as mole rats and bamboo rats, lose their distinction when their lineages are traced far back in time. Whether recognized as the family Muridae or the superfamily Muroidea, the living members of these 18 groups show an impressive range of variation in body form, locomotion, and ecology.

FORM AND FUNCTION

The body form of tree squirrels may be the model for the earliest, and presumably generalized, rodents (genus *Paramys*). With their ability to adhere to bark with their claws, squirrels adeptly scamper up tree trunks, run along branches, and leap to adjacent trees; but they are equally agile on the ground, and some are capable swimmers. Burrowers are also represented in the form of long-tailed ground squirrels.

The widely recognizable eastern gray squirrel (Sciurus carolinensis). Hope Lourie Killcoyne

The specialized body forms of other kinds of rodents tie them closer to particular locomotor patterns and ecologies. Some strictly arboreal species have a prehensile tail; others glide from tree to tree supported by fur-covered membranes between appendages. Highly specialized fossorial (burrowing) rodents, including blind mole rats, blesmols, and ground squirrels, are cylindrical and furry with protruding, strong incisors, small eyes and ears, and large forefeet bearing powerful digging claws. Semiaquatic rodents such as beavers, muskrats, nutrias, and water rats possess specialized traits allowing them to forage in aquatic habitats yet den in ground burrows. Terrestrial leaping species, such as kangaroo rats, jumping mice, gerbils, and jerboas, have short forelimbs, long and powerful hind limbs and feet, and a long tail used for balance. Body forms of some rodents converge on those in nonrodent orders, resembling shrews, moles, hares, pikas, pigs, or small forest deer. There is also convergence between distantly related groups of rodents in particular body forms and associated natural histories.

Regardless of body form, though, all rodents share the same basic tools that, as mammologists Louise Emmons and Francois Feer noted, "can be used to cut, pry, slice, gouge, dig, stab, or delicately hold like a pair of tweezers; they can cut grass, open nuts, kill animal prey, dig tunnels, and fell large trees."

EVOLUTION

As documented by fossils, the evolutionary history of rodents extends back 56 million years to the Late Paleocene Epoch in North America. Those species, however, are considered to have originated in Eurasia, so the origin of the order Rodentia is certainly older. However, lack of fossil evidence prior to the Late Paleocene makes the understanding of evolutionary relationships between rodents above the familial level a continuing quest. Specialists agree with the definitions of most families, but they historically have disagreed, and still do, about the arrangement of families into larger groups—namely, suborders. Past classifications either have omitted suborders altogether and grouped the families into superfamilies or have grouped the families into 2, 7, 11, or 16 suborders. Some specialists recognize just two suborders, Sciurognathi and Hystricognathi, which were proposed in 1899 and were based on conformation of the lower jaw. But any arrangement is simply a hypothesis of relationships between rodent families that is continually being tested by discovery of new fossils, reanalyses of data from conventional sources, and new analyses of data from many different, unrelated sources.

CHAPTER 2
RATS AND SIMILAR FORMS

The term *rat* is generally and indiscriminately applied to numerous members of several rodent families having bodies longer than about 12 cm, or about 5 inches. (Smaller thin-tailed rodents are just as often indiscriminately referred to as mice.) In scientific usage, *rat* applies to any of 56 thin-tailed, medium-sized rodent species in the genus *Rattus* native to continental Asia and the adjacent islands of Southeast Asia eastward to the Australia-New Guinea region. A few species have spread far beyond their native range in close association with people. The brown rat, *Rattus norvegicus* (also called the Norway rat), and the

Norway rat (Rattus norvegicus). John H. Gerard

house rat, *R. rattus* (also called the black rat, ship rat, or roof rat), live virtually everywhere that human populations have settled; the house rat is predominant in warmer climates, and the brown rat dominates in temperate regions, especially urban areas. Most likely originating in Asia, the brown rat reached Europe in the mid-1500s and North America around 1750. The house rat most likely originated in India.

Brown and house rats exploit human food resources, eating and contaminating stored grains and killing poultry. They have been responsible for the depletion or extinction of native species of small mammals, birds, and reptiles, especially on oceanic islands. Both the brown and house rat have been implicated in the spread of 40 diseases among humans, including bubonic plague, food poisoning, schistosomiasis, murine typhus, tularemia, and leptospirosis. On the other hand, the brown rat has been used in laboratories worldwide for medical, genetic, and basic biological research aimed at maintaining and improving human health. Rats are also kept as pets.

GENERAL FEATURES

Rats are generally slender with a pointed head, large eyes, and prominent, thinly furred ears. They have moderately long legs and long, sharp claws. The bald soles of their narrow hind feet possess fleshy pads of variable size, depending on species. The brown rat has a larger body than the house rat, and its tail is shorter relative to the body. The brown rat also has thicker fur and 12 pairs of mammae (mammary glands) instead of 10. Tail length among rats ranges from shorter than body length to appreciably longer. The tail appears smooth and bald but is actually covered with very short, fine hairs. In a few species, these hairs become longer toward the tip, which gives the tail a slightly tufted appearance. As with any large group of rodents, body size varies within the genus. Most species are about the size of Hoffman's rat (*R. hoffmanni*), native to the Indonesian islands of Sulawesi (Celebes) and weighing 95 to 240 grams (3.4 to 8.5 ounces), with a body length of 17 to 21 cm (6.7 to 8.3 inches) and a tail about as long. One of the smaller species is Osgood's rat (*R. osgoodi*) of southern Vietnam, with a body 12 to 17 cm (4.7 to 6.7 inches) long and a somewhat shorter tail. At the larger extreme is the Sulawesian white-tailed rat (*R. xanthurus*), measuring 19 to 27 cm (about 7.5 to 10.6 inches) long with a tail of 26 to 34 cm (10.2 to 13.4 inches).

Like Hoffman's rat, most species have a moderately short, soft, and dense coat. In some species the coat may be thicker and longer, somewhat woolly, or long and coarse; in others, such as the Sulawesian white-tailed rat and the Sikkim rat (*R. remotus*) of India, long and slender guard hairs resembling whiskers extend 4 to 6 cm (1.6 to 2.4 inches) beyond the coat on the back and rump. Very few *Rattus* species have spiny fur. Hoffman's rat also exhibits the basic colour pattern seen in the genus—upperparts of brownish yellow peppered with black to dark brown and speckled with buff and underparts from silvery gray to dark gray, sometimes suffused with buff tones. Tail, ears, and feet are dark brown. As with fur texture, colour is variable. The Sikkim rat has brownish upperparts and a pure white underside; the Himalayan field rat (*R. nitidus*) has a brown back, gray underparts, and feet of pearly white. Others have very dark fur, such as the Mentawai rat (*R. lugens*) native to islands off the west coast of Sumatra. It has brownish black upperparts and a grayish black belly. Although the tail is uniformly gray to dark brown in most rats (sometimes nearly black), a few species show one of two bicoloured patterns: brown on the tail's entire upper surface with a paler tone or pure white on the undersurface, as in the Himalayan field rat and the Turkestan rat (*R. turkestanicus*), or brown all around the basal third to half of the tail with the rest uniformly white, as in Hoogerwerf's rat (*R. hoogerwerfi*) and the white-tailed rat of Sulawesi.

NATURAL HISTORY

In their natural habitats rats are primarily nocturnal—the brown rat is a prominent exception, being active day and night in both urban and rural environments. All rats are terrestrial, and many are also arboreal. The Sulawesian white-tailed rat is an excellent climber and exhibits the classic combination of arboreal traits within *Rattus*: a very long tail relative to body length, extremely long guard hairs over the back and rump, and wide hind feet with prominent, fleshy footpads. This rodent dens among the roots of large trees (generally strangler figs) and forages high in the crowns of understory and canopy trees. By contrast, those species having a tail considerably shorter than body length, short guard hairs over the back and rump, and inconspicuous pads on the soles of their hind feet tend to be primarily ground-dwelling. Most rats can swim; species with thick and somewhat woolly fur generally swim well, and some are adept swimmers that forage in aquatic environments. The brown rat, for example, has a terrestrial rat's characteristic morphology and is a comparatively poor climber, but it has dense fur and readily enters lakes and streams and sewers to hunt for fish, invertebrates, or other food. The house rat, on the other hand, is extremely agile above the ground, being able to climb and run along narrow branches and wires.

Rats are thought to eat everything, a conception that comes from familiarity with the highly adaptable brown rat and house rat, but diet actually differs according to species and habitat. Where it lives with humans, the house rat does consume nearly anything digestible, especially stored grains. The brown rat is basically omnivorous but prefers a carnivorous diet, aggressively pursuing a wide variety of prey including shrimp, snails, mussels, insects, bird eggs and young, amphibians, eels, fish, pheasant, pigeons, poultry, rabbits, and carrion. Many rainforest species, including the Sulawesian white-tailed rat and Hoffman's rat, eat only fruit and the seeds within, but some, such as the Philippine forest rat (*R. everetti*), also eat insects and worms. Other tropical species, such as the rice field rat (*R. argentiventer*) and Malayan field rat (*R. tiomanicus*), primarily consume the insects, snails, slugs, and other invertebrates found in habitats of forest patches, secondary growth, scrubby and fallow fields, palm plantations, and rice fields.

Some rats excavate burrows or build their nests beneath boulders, rotting tree trunks, or other kinds of shelter on the forest floor; they may also shelter in deep rock crevices or caves and in dwellings from small village huts to large city buildings. Rat reproduction has been most intensively studied in the brown rat. This prolific rodent reaches sexual maturity at three months and may produce up to 12 litters of 2 to 22 young (8 or 9 is usual) per year, with peaks in the spring and autumn and a gestation period of 21 to 26 days. Breeding occurs throughout the year in many tropical species but in others may be restricted to wet seasons or summer months. Litter sizes in tropical forest species tend to be much smaller (one to six), and seasonal breeders, particularly in Australian habitats, produce significantly fewer annual litters.

CLASSIFICATION AND PALEONTOLOGY

Members of the genus *Rattus* are native to temperate and tropical continental Asia, the Australia–New Guinea region, and islands between those landmasses. Five clusters of species within the genus are recognized by some authorities.

The *norvegicus* group, consisting only of the brown rat, may have originated in northern or northeastern China.

Most of the 20 species in the *rattus* group are indigenous to subtropical and tropical Asia from peninsular India to southeastern China, Southeast Asia, Taiwan, some islands in the Philippines, and Sulawesi. They live in lowland and montane rainforests, scrublands, agricultural and fallow fields, and human structures. In addition to the house rat, the distributions of four other species (*R. argentiventer*, *R. nitidus*, *R. exulans*, and *R. tanezumi*) extend outside continental Southeast Asia, from the Sunda Shelf to New Guinea and beyond to some Pacific islands, and most likely represent introductions facilitated by human activities.

The 19 species in the "Australia–New Guinea" group are native to Australia, New Guinea and adjacent islands, and the Moluccan and Lesser Sunda Islands between Australia–New Guinea and continental Southeast Asia. They occupy habitats including sandy flats, open grasslands, and grassy areas within forest, heaths, savannas, and tropical rainforests.

The *xanthurus* group comprises five species indigenous to Sulawesi and nearby Peleng Island, where they inhabit tropical rainforest formations at all elevations.

There are 11 species whose relationships are unresolved. These have endemic ranges from peninsular India through Southeast Asia to the Philippines. Most now live, or once lived, in tropical rainforests; two species are extinct.

Rattus species belong to the subfamily Murinae (Old World rats and mice) of the "true" mouse and rat family, Muridae, within the order Rodentia. Among their closest living relatives are the bandicoot rats (genera *Bandicota* and *Nesokia*). Information about the evolutionary history of the genus is scanty; fossils from the Pleistocene Epoch (2,600,000 to 11,700 years ago) in Asia, Java, and Australia represent the oldest extinct species of *Rattus*.

TYPES OF RATS

Although the overwhelming majority of rat species are primarily nocturnal in their native habitat, some groups are more nocturnal than others. For descriptive purposes, it is useful to divide rats into those groups that are active at night and those that are not exclusively nocturnal.

NOCTURNAL GROUPS

Most rats are exclusively nocturnal or predominantly so. This category includes such widely distributed groups as the chinchilla rat from South America, the maned rat from East Africa, and the bandicoot rat of Southeast Asia, Taiwan, and the island of Java.

An example of a giant pouched rat, possibly Cricetomys emini. Jane Burton-Bruce Coleman Inc.

AFRICAN POUCHED RATS

The name *African pouched rat* (subfamily Cricetomyinae) can be applied to any of five species of African rodents. African pouched rats are characterized by cheek pouches that are used for carrying food back to their burrows, where it is eaten or stored. All are terrestrial and have gray to brown coats with white or gray underparts, but the three genera differ in size, behaviour, and geographic distribution. The smaller species are sometimes called pouched mice.

The two species of giant pouched rat (genus *Cricetomys*) are hunted in the wild and eaten by native peoples. Gentle animals, they are easily tamed and raised in captivity and thus have been studied to determine their marketability as a reliable source of food. Both species (*C. gambianus* and *C. emini*) are large, weighing nearly 3 kg (6.6 pounds) and having bodies up to 42 cm (16 inches) long. Their long heads have large ears; the scantily haired tail is longer than the body and is white on the terminal half. Predominantly nocturnal, giant pouched rats are omnivorous and are found throughout sub-Saharan Africa, except for southern South Africa. Habitats in which they live include forests and woodlands, as well as gardens, orchards (where they climb fruit trees during the day), and sometimes houses. Although these rats occasionally den in abandoned termite mounds, they live mostly in burrows dug in moist and shady areas. Litter size ranges from one to five.

The short-tailed pouched rats (genus *Saccostomus*) are small and thickset, weighing about 75 grams (2.6 ounces) and having bodies up to 18 cm (7 inches) long and much shorter tails. Both species (*S. campestris* and *S. mearnsi*) are soft-furred, nocturnal, and slow-moving. They feed primarily on seeds during wet periods but also eat insects during drought. Although they can excavate their own burrows, they also use dens made by other animals, as well as holes among tree roots and rock piles. Short-tailed pouched rats living in environments where the temperature is highly variable go spontaneously into torpor. These rats usually inhabit savannas and natural grasslands from eastern to southern Africa, but they sometimes can be found living in or near cultivated land. Litter size ranges from 1 to 10.

The long-tailed pouched rat (*Beamys hindei*), also nocturnal, is a nimble climber. Medium-sized, it weighs up to 97 grams (3.4 ounces) and has a body up to 16 cm (6.3 inches) long and a scantily haired tail about as long as the head and body. It constructs burrows in soft sandy soil along the coasts of southern Kenya and Tanzania and inland southward to northeastern Zambia. This species lives in a variety of forest habitats and open woodlands and is occasionally found in fallow agricultural fields and cassava plantations. The long-tailed pouched rat eats seeds and fruit and bears litters of four to seven young. Uncommon and dependent upon wooded habitats, this rodent has been made vulnerable to extinction by deforestation.

African pouched rats constitute the subfamily Cricetomyinae of the mouse and rat family Muridae within the order Rodentia. Although *Beamys* and *Cricetomys* are not represented by fossils, preserved fragments of *Saccostomus* provide evidence that its evolutionary history dates back three million to five million years during the Pliocene Epoch.

American Spiny Rats

There are at least 80 species of American spiny rats (family Echimyidae). American spiny rats are medium-sized

Central and South American rodents that have a bristly coat of flat flexible spines, although a few have soft fur. Like "true" rats and mice (family Muridae), spiny rats are slender and have short limbs, small hairless ears, large eyes, and either pointed or blunt noses with long whiskers. The tail breaks off easily when pulled, and many individuals thus have stubby or missing tails. When intact, tails range from less than half the body length to much longer; they may be thinly or densely haired and are sometimes patterned.

American spiny rats weigh from 130 to 900 grams (4.6 ounces to 2 pounds) and have a body 11 to 48 cm (4.3 to 18.9 inches) long. Their coats show an impressive range of colours and markings. At one extreme is the plain punare (*Thrichomys apereoides*), with dull brown upperparts and grayish white underparts. At the other extreme is the painted tree rat (*Callistomys pictus*), whose whitish body has a wide, glossy black stripe on the neck and head and a saddle pattern extending from the shoulders and across the upper arms over the back and rump; its black hairy tail is tipped with white above and golden yellow below.

During the day American spiny rats shelter in burrows, tree hollows, or brush piles, or among rocks and tree roots. Some are arboreal and some terrestrial; among the terrestrial species, some burrow and others do not. Their diet includes

White-faced spiny tree rat (Echimys chrysurus). Warren Garst—Tom Stack and Associates

leaves and shoots of plants, nuts, fruit, fungi, and insects, although the American bamboo rats (genera *Dactylomys* and *Kannabateomys*) prefer the shoots, leaves, and stems of bamboo.

Spiny rats range from southern Mexico through South America to Paraguay and southeastern Brazil. Owl's spiny rat (*Carterodon sulcidens*), Lund's spiny rats (genus *Clyomys*), the guiara (*Euryzygomatomys spinosus*), and the punare (*T. apereoides*) live in the savannas of eastern and southern Brazil and Paraguay. The others inhabit tropical rainforests throughout Central and South America.

The 18 surviving genera belong to three subfamilies of the family Echimyidae, in the suborder Hystricognatha within the order Rodentia. All species within four West Indian genera are now extinct, most within historical times: Cuban and Hispaniolan cave rats (*Boromys* and *Heteropsomys*), edible rats (*Brotomys*), and the Puerto Rican Corozal rat (*Puertoricomys corozalis*). These form a fifth subfamily in Echimyidae that may be more closely related to the exotic hutias (chapter 5). Fossils representing a wide array of extinct species and genera trace the evolutionary history of Echimyidae back to the Late Oligocene Epoch (23.8 million to 28.5 million years ago) in South America.

BAMBOO RATS

Bamboo rats are burrowing, slow-moving, nocturnal rodents. The four living species are native to Asia. Each one is characterized by a robust, cylindrical body, small ears and eyes, and short, stout legs. The three species of *Rhizomys* are 23 to 50 cm (9.1 to 19.7 inches) long with a short and bald or sparsely haired tail (5 to 20 cm [2 to 7.9 inches]). Fur on the upperparts is soft and dense or harsh and scanty, coloured slate gray to brownish gray with a paler underside. The lesser bamboo rat (genus *Cannomys*) is smaller—15 to 27 cm (5.9 to 10.6 inches) long, excluding the 6- to 8-cm (2.4- to 3.1-inch) tail. Its long, dense fur ranges from chestnut brown to a bright pale gray.

The genus *Rhizomys* is found in bamboo-covered hills and mountains from Indochina to the Malay Peninsula and Sumatra, where the rats bear litters of three to five young. The lesser bamboo rat, on the other hand, inhabits uplands from southeastern Nepal through southern China and Myanmar (Burma) to northwestern Vietnam and Thailand; its litter size is one to two. All bamboo rats are a food source for the native peoples of these countries.

Bamboo rats dig with their incisor teeth, using the head and claws to remove loosened soil. *Rhizomys* species construct extensive burrow systems among roots of dense bamboo stands, where they feed primarily on bamboo roots. At night they forage above ground for fruit, seeds, and nest materials, even climbing the bamboo and cutting sections that they carry to their burrows and eat later. They have also been reported to venture onto plantations to feed on roots of sugarcane and cassava. The lesser bamboo rat digs deep tunnels in the rocky ground of mountain meadows, forests, and even gardens; its diet consists of a wide variety of plant material. It has been found on tea plantations, but the extent of the damage it causes is unknown.

In addition to the single species of lesser bamboo rat (*C. badius*), the three *Rhizomys* bamboo rats are the Chinese bamboo rat (*R. sinensis*), the hoary bamboo rat (*R. pruinosus*), and the large bamboo rat (*R. sumatrensis*). All bamboo rats belong to the subfamily Rhyzomyinae, which includes their closest living relatives, the African mole rats (genus *Tachyoryctes*). Subfamily Rhyzomyinae is classified within the family Muridae (rats and mice) of the order Rodentia. The lineage of today's *Rhizomys* species can be traced to extinct genera represented by fossils found in Pakistan,

India, and China dating from 10,000,000 to 500,000 years ago (late Miocene to Pleistocene Epoch).

BANDICOOT RATS

Bandicoot rats are also native to Asia, and the five species in this group are closely associated with human populations. The greater bandicoot rat (*Bandicota indica*) is the largest, weighing 0.5 to 1 kg (1.1 to 2.2 pounds). The shaggy, blackish brown body is 19 to 33 cm (7.5 to 13 inches) long, not including a scantily haired tail of about the same length. Greater bandicoot rats are found on the Indian subcontinent and throughout Indochina; additional populations on the Malay Peninsula, Taiwan, and Java probably represent inadvertent or intentional human introductions.

Greater bandicoot rat (Bandicota indica). Painting by Don Meighan

The lesser bandicoot rat (*B. bengalensis*) and Savile's bandicoot rat (*B. savilei*) have dark brown or brownish gray body fur, weigh up to 350 grams (12.3 ounces), and measure up to 40 cm (15.7 inches) long including their brown tails. The lesser bandicoot rat is found on the Indian subcontinent, Sri Lanka (formerly Ceylon), and Myanmar and has been introduced on Pinang Island off the western coast of the Malay Peninsula, northern Sumatra, eastern Java, Saudi Arabia, and Patta Island in Kenya. Savile's bandicoot rat, on the other hand, occurs only on the mainland of Southeast Asia. These three terrestrial species are nocturnal or active at twilight, constructing burrows where they nest and where they bear their litters, which number from 2 to 18. They subsist on grains, fruit, and invertebrates and are destructive to cultivated crops. The lesser bandicoot rat, an especially aggressive burrower, has been reported to make tunnels in the concrete cellars of rice warehouses in Calcutta.

Except for one population of Savile's bandicoot rat found in the grass beneath a teak forest in Thailand, no population of bandicoot rats has been recorded in a native habitat. Instead, bandicoot rats now inhabit cultivated land, and the lesser bandicoot rat also thrives in urban buildings. Adaptation to tropical forests was probably not a part of their evolutionary history, as forest-dwelling species of rats cannot make the transition from pristine forest to cultivated field and are rarely associated with humans. Original habitats for the bandicoot rats were probably ecologically similar to the man-made environments where they are now found, as many planted crops or fallow fields resemble native grassland, rice fields are marshlike, and orchards may approximate scrub or open forest.

Of the two species of *Nesokia*, the short-tailed bandicoot rat, or pest rat (*N. indica*), is almost the size of the lesser bandicoot rat, with soft brown fur and a short tail.

Its range extends from northern Bangladesh through Central Asia to northeastern Egypt and also north of the Himalayas from Turkmenistan to western China. Inhabiting cultivated fields and natural grasslands in generally arid regions, the rats excavate extensive tunnels just below the surface and push up mounds of earth at intervals that conceal entrances and exits. They forage on bulbs and succulent roots, rarely emerging above ground, and cause extensive damage to grain crops. *N. bunnii*, however, is as large as the greater bandicoot rat, with thick fur and a very long tail relative to body length. An excellent swimmer, it lives in natural marshes at the confluence of the Tigris and Euphrates rivers in southeastern Iraq and builds nests on reed platforms above water level.

All bandicoot rats belong to the subfamily Murinae of the family Muridae within the order Rodentia.

CHINCHILLA RATS

All six extant species of chinchilla rats are native to South America. Superficially, chinchilla rats resemble chinchillas but are more ratlike in body form. Chinchilla rats have short limbs, large eyes, and large, rounded ears. The forefeet have four digits, the hind feet five, and the hairless, padded soles are covered with tiny tubercles (nodules) that provide traction on bark or rocks. *Abrocoma* species have small claws, but claws are large and curved in *Cuscomys*; the second digits of both genera are hollowed out underneath. Stiff hairs, possibly used as grooming combs, project over the middle three toes. *Abrocoma* species are medium-sized rodents weighing up to 350 grams (12.3 ounces) with a body 17 to 23 cm (6.7 to 9.1 inches) long and a densely haired tail of 6 to 18 cm (2.4 to 7 inches). *Cuscomys* is larger, weighing 0.91 kg (2 pounds), with a body length of 35 cm (13.8 inches) and a long, furred, two-coloured tail (26 cm [10.2 inches]). Chinchilla rats' long, soft, dense fur ranges from silvery to brownish gray on the upperparts with white, gray, or brownish underparts.

The four *Abrocoma* species are primarily nocturnal and terrestrial. They den in rock crevices or burrows, are agile rock climbers, and climb shrubs and small trees. Their diet consists of leaves, buds, and stems of shrubs. Several are usually seen in close proximity to one another, perhaps forming small colonies. Some species build latrines up to 3 metres (10 feet) high that project from rock crevices and are composed of feces glued together by urine and other liquids. These structures eventually become as hard as rock.

Of the two *Cuscomys* species, *C. oblativa* is represented only by remains from an Inca burial site at Machu Picchu, although there is speculation that the species may still live nearby. The other species, *C. ashaninka* (named for the Ashaninka people of the region), appears to be arboreal, and little is known of its habits. It was first described in 1999 from a single specimen obtained at 3,370 metres (about 11,000 feet) in the cloud forest of southern Peru, about 200 km (124 miles) from Machu Picchu.

Chinchilla rats occur in the Andes Mountains from southern Peru to west-central Argentina, extending from coastal foothills up to the Altiplano, a region in southeastern Peru and western Bolivia. *Abrocoma* species prefer rocky areas covered by brushy vegetation and grass or open, rockless scrublands. Bennett's chinchilla rat (*A. bennetti*) occupies scrub habitats in central Chile from near the coast up to 1,200 metres (about 3,900 feet) above sea level, occurring along with the degu (*Octodon degus*). The two animals are approximately the same size, and mothers and young of both species have been found in the same nest burrows. *A. boliviensis* inhabits rocky, shrubby areas at altitudes of about 2,500 metres (8,200 feet) in central Bolivia. The ashy chinchilla rat (*A. cinerea*) lives only in the Altiplano, between 3,700 and 5,000 metres (12,000 and

16,400 feet), from southeastern Peru to northern Chile and Argentina. *A. vaccarum* is known from rocky cliff faces at 1,880 metres (about 6,200 feet) above sea level in west-central Argentina.

Chinchilla rats belong to the family Abrocomidae of the suborder Hystricognatha within the order Rodentia. Their closest living relatives are the family Chinchillidae (chinchillas and viscachas). The evolutionary history of Abrocomidae dates from the Early Miocene Epoch (23.8 million to 16.4 million years ago) in Argentina.

CLOUD RATS

Cloud rats, also known as cloudrunners, are slow-moving, nocturnal, tree-dwelling rodents found only in Philippine forests. There are six species. Giant cloud rats belong to the genus *Phloeomys* (two species), whereas bushy-tailed cloud rats are classified in the genus *Crateromys* (four species).

Luzon bushy-tailed cloud rat (Crateromys schadenbergi). Painting by Don Meighan

Giant Cloud Rats

Also called slender-tailed cloud rats, both species of *Phloeomys* live on the island of Luzon and weigh from 1.5 to more than 2 kg (3.3 to 4.4 pounds). Their bodies range in length from 30 to 50 cm (12 to 20 inches), not including a furred tail that is about as long as the body. *Phloeomys pallidus*, found in northern Luzon, has long, dense, soft fur of cream or pale gray interrupted by black or brown markings. It is easily distinguished from *P. cumingi*, which has short, dark brown fur. *P. cumingi* lives in southern Luzon and on the offshore island of Catanduanes. Both species are found from lowlands to mountains, where they nest in hollow trees and feed on tender young leaves. One young per year is usual.

Bushy-Tailed Cloud Rats

Three of the four species of *Crateromys* were first described by scientists during the 1980s and '90s, the most recent being the Panay Island cloud rat (*C. heaneyi*) in 1996. Additional undiscovered species may live on other Philippine islands. All cloud rats are intimately tied to old-growth tropical forests, and most populations are in danger owing to overhunting and deforestation. Three of the four *Crateromys* species have long, soft, thick fur that can be wavy or straight. The long, bushy tail is a unique feature among Old World rats and mice (subfamily Murinae). The Luzon bushy-tailed cloud rat (*C. schadenbergi*) is fairly common in the mountain forests of northern Luzon, but this is the only island on which it is found. It is the largest of the genus, with a body length of 35 to 39 cm (13.8 to 15.4 inches), and is polymorphic in fur colour—that is, individuals may be all black, all white, or some pattern of black, white, and brown.

The bushy-tailed cloud rat of Panay Island (*C. heaneyi*) is a smaller, brown version of *C. schadenbergi* measuring 25 to 35 cm (about 9.8 to 13.8 inches) long with a tail longer than its body. The Dinigat bushy-tailed cloud rat (*C. australis*) is about the same size as *C. heaneyi* and is found only on Dinagat Island, north of

Mindanao. It has tawny fur on the head and back and an orange-brown belly.

With a body length of 25 cm (9.8 inches), the Ilin bushy-tailed cloud rat (*C. paulus*) is the smallest of the group, with short, coarse, brown fur, a cream-coloured underside, and a short, hairy, tricoloured tail. It was found on Ilin Island, off the southern coast of Mindoro, but may already be extinct on Ilin because of extensive deforestation.

Ecological information exists for only the species from Luzon and Panay. The Luzon bushy-tailed cloud rat inhabits oak and pine forests, eating pine buds and bark and building stick nests in the crowns of trees. The Panay Island bushy-tailed cloud rat dens in tree trunks, in cavities among tree roots, and inside large tree ferns. Its diet consists of leaves, fruits, and seeds. Single young have been reported for both species, but pairs of young have been observed among the Panay Island species.

All cloud rats belong to the "true" mouse and rat family Muridae within the order Rodentia. They are closely related to Luzon tree rats (*Carpomys*) and hairy-tailed rats (*Batomys*), both of which are also endemic to the Philippines.

Maned Rats

The maned rat (*Lophiomys imhausi*), which is also known as the crested rat, is a long-haired and bushy-tailed East African rodent that resembles a porcupine. It is named for its mane of long, coarse black-and-white-banded hairs that begins at the top of the head and extends beyond the base of the tail. The maned rat is a large rodent (up to 2.7 kg, or 6 pounds) with a long body (25 to 36 cm, or 10 to 14 inches) and a tail 14 to 21 cm (5.5 to 8.3 inches) long. The limbs are short and the ears small. Its long, thick, silky fur is broken up by black or white stripes and blotches, and the underparts are covered in short grayish white fur.

KANGAROO RATS

Kangaroo rat (Dipodomys). Anthony Mercieca/Root Resources

There are 22 known species of kangaroo rats (genus *Dipodomys*). All are bipedal North American desert rodents with a tufted tail. Kangaroo rats have large heads and eyes, short forelimbs, and very long hind legs and feet. Fur-lined external cheek pouches open alongside the mouth and can be everted for cleaning. Kangaroo rats are considered medium-sized, weighing 35 to 180 grams (1.2 to 6.3 ounces), with a body 10 to 20 cm (4 to 8 inches) long and a tail of similar length. Fur is soft, dense, and silky and ranges in colour from sandy to dark brown with white facial markings, a white strip on each hip, and white underparts. The hairy tail bears a prominent white or brown tuft and balances the body during movement. Kangaroo rats hop on their hind legs up to 2 metres (6.6 feet) at a bound and use their forelegs only when traversing short distances. They keep their fur clean by bathing in fine sand; without this relief, they develop body sores and matted fur.

Kangaroo rats excavate burrows either below the surface of the ground or within large mounds of earth; some species construct nests. Although they are desert dwellers, most species are good swimmers. They seldom drink water, obtaining sufficient moisture from their diet of seeds, stems, buds, fruit, and insects. Chisel-toothed kangaroo rats (*Dipodomys microps*) are one of the few mammals that can eat the salty leaves of the saltbush, which is common in the Great Basin. Peeling the skin from each leaf with their lower front teeth, they consume the underlying layers, which are rich in water and nutrients. Kangaroo rats forage at night and transport food in their cheek pouches to store either in the burrow or in shallow pits nearby. No kangaroo rats hibernate; instead, they depend upon cached food during the winter. After about a month's gestation, one or more litters per year of two to five young are born.

Found in western North America from southern Canada to southern Mexico, kangaroo rats prefer well-drained sandy or gravelly soils in a variety of open, sparsely vegetated, hot and dry habitats such as chaparral and sagebrush, desert grassland, mixed grass- and scrubland, and piñon-juniper woodland. The Texas kangaroo rat (*D. elator*) constructs burrows in disturbed areas along fencerows and pasture roads and around stock corrals, barns, and grain-storage facilities. Recently, accelerated transformation of desert habitats by residential and agricultural development has imperiled several species of kangaroo rat.

Kangaroo rats are classified in the family Heteromyidae (Greek: "other mice," or "different mice") rather than with the "true" mice (family Muridae) within the order Rodentia. Their closest living relatives are kangaroo mice and pocket mice, both of which are also heteromyids. Pocket gophers (family Geomyidae) are related to the family Heteromyidae. The kangaroo rat's evolutionary history began during the Late Miocene Epoch (11.2 million to 5.3 million years ago) in North America.

The mane is set off from the rest of the coat by a broad white-bordered band of hairs covering a glandular area of skin, and the mane is erected when the animal is disturbed.

The maned rat is found in dry forests of southern Sudan, in Ethiopia, and in isolated mountain woodlands of Tanzania. In Ethiopia it lives in a variety of habitats from sea level to 3,300 metres (10,800 feet). The natural history of this unique rodent has not been thoroughly studied. It is nocturnal and a good climber, but it moves slowly. During the day it dens among rocks, in holes of dead trees, among tree roots, and in sides of ravines. Leaves, fruits, and tender shoots constitute its diet in the wild, but root vegetables, cereals, meat, and insects have been accepted in captivity. The maned rat sits on its haunches when eating, manipulating food with its front feet. Apparently one young per litter is usual.

Maned, or crested, rat (Lophiomys imhausi). P.W. Hay from The National Audubon Society Collection/Photo Researchers

The maned rat is the sole living representative of the subfamily Lophiomyinae in the mouse family (Muridae) within the order Rodentia. Fragments of a cranium found in Israel suggest that its present geographic distribution is part of a more extensive former range, and it may still exist on the Arabian Peninsula. Past diversity of the genus was greater as well, as indicated by fossil fragments from Morocco representing two additional species from the Pliocene Epoch (5.3 million to 2.6 million years ago). A possible ancestor of the maned rat (*Protolophiomys ibericus*) was discovered in six-million- to seven-million-year-old deposits of southern Spain. Although most of these fossils are cranial fragments, they are easily recognized as relatives of the maned rat by a granulated, bony caplike growth over the top of the entire skull — a structure unique to members of the subfamily Lophiomyinae.

RICE RATS

The 36 species of rice rats (genus *Oryzomys*) are found from the United States southward through tropical and portions of subtropical South America. Rice rats are small, nocturnal rodents that have soft fur, with tawny to grayish brown upperparts and paler underparts. Their tails are sparsely haired and vary in length depending upon the species. Body size also varies. Among the smallest is *Oryzomys alfaroi*, from southern Mexico to western Ecuador, with a body up to 12 cm (4.7 inches) long and a slightly shorter tail; among the largest is *O. angouya*, found in eastern Brazil, Paraguay, and southern Argentina, with a body length up to 20 cm (7.9 inches) and a much longer tail.

When the rice rat genus was first named and described scientifically in 1858, it included only the marsh rice rat (*O. palustris*), a pest of rice plantations in the southeastern United States during the colonial period. This species is now most commonly found in coastal marshes (an environment similar to inundated rice fields) and also occurs in forest clearings of grass and scrub as well as wet meadows in foothills of the Appalachian Mountains. One of the few nonforest species in the genus, marsh rice rats are good swimmers and nimble climbers in marsh grasses or shrubs, where they construct globular nests. They are opportunistic feeders, eating seeds, succulent parts of grasses, invertebrates, small vertebrates, and carrion.

Additional species will undoubtedly be discovered as South American rodents become better studied. Two were described as recently as 1998—one from Ecuador in the Andes Mountains, the other from northeastern Brazil. Nearly all members of the genus live in tropical and subtropical forests. Many occur only at low elevations, but a few are restricted to cloud forests in the mountains of southern Mexico, Central America, and the Andes. Certain rice rats are indigenous to particular biogeographic regions; for example, *O. megacephalus* and *O. yunganus* are restricted to lowland tropical rainforests of the Amazon Basin, and *O. bolivaris* is found only in very wet tropical forests of the Trans-Andean region. Much has been learned about the ecologies of some species with extensive geographic ranges and high population densities, such as *O. megacephalus*. Others, such as Thomas's rice rat (*O. dimidiatus*) from southeastern Nicaragua, are rare and are found only in one or two places, and most aspects of their natural histories are unknown.

Several related genera are also sometimes referred to as rice rats, including arboreal rice rats (*Oecomys*), dark rice rats (*Melanomys*), small rice rats (*Microryzomys*), and pygmy rice rats (*Oligoryzomys*), among others. All belong to the subfamily Sigmodontinae of the "true" mouse and rat family Muridae within the order Rodentia.

Woodrats

Woodrats (genus *Neotoma*) are medium-sized North and Central American rodents. Some of the 20 known species are commonly known as "packrats" for their characteristic accumulation of food and debris in or near their dens. These collections, called "middens," may include bones, sticks, dry manure, shiny metal objects, and innumerable items discarded by or stolen from humans.

The bushy-tailed woodrat (*Neotoma cinerea*), often called a packrat, is among the largest and most common woodrats, weighing up to 600 grams (about 1.3 pounds) and having a body length of up to 25 cm (nearly 10 inches). Its slightly shorter tail is longhaired and bushy, which is unique within the genus. The Arizona woodrat (*N. devia*) is one of the smallest, weighing less than 132 grams (4.7

ounces) and having a body length of up to 15 cm (5.9 inches). Its tail, measuring up to 14 cm (5.5 inches) long, is more typical in being densely haired but not bushy. Woodrats' eyes are large, their protruding ears are nearly bald, and their feet are white. The long, thick, soft fur varies among species from gray to reddish brown above and from white to rust-coloured on the underparts. Some populations of the desert woodrat (*N. lepida*) and the white-throated woodrat (*N. albigula*) are black (melanistic).

Woodrats are nocturnal and active year-round. Generally solitary, they range from the Yukon and westernmost Northwest Territories throughout most of the United States south to western Honduras. They populate a broad spectrum of habitats, including desert plateaus and mountains, the southern Great Plains, and many

White-throated wood rat (Neotoma albigula). G.C. Kelley/Photo Researchers, Inc.

types of forest (eastern deciduous, piñon-juniper, coniferous, boreal, and tropical thorn and scrub). All woodrats
are vegetarian, and three species exhibit dietary special-
ization: Stephen's woodrat (*N. stephensi*) subsists almost
entirely on juniper sprigs, and *N. albigula* and *N. lepida* feed
mostly on prickly pear, cholla cacti, and yucca plants.

At the simple extreme of woodrat nest construction
is that of the Allegheny woodrat (*N. magister*). Although
it is merely a cup made of plants, the rat protects it with
a small pile of sticks among boulders on a cliff ledge or
inside a cave. The most elaborate configuration is the huge
stick nest of the dusky-footed woodrat (*N. fuscipes*), which
can be more than a metre (3.3 feet) high and is built on the
ground, on rocky slopes, or in tree canopies. Other woodrats live in moderately large structures built at the bases
of cacti, bushes, or trees, in caves, on rock-strewn slopes,
or on ledges. Structures in arid sites protected from rain
become very hard owing to the high mineral content of
the woodrat's urine, which is used as cement. Such middens remain intact for thousands of years. By analyzing
the preserved plants in these ancient dens, ecologists and
paleontologists can reconstruct plant communities and
climate over the last 40,000 years in the southwestern
United States.

Woodrats are usually common within their ranges,
but Allegheny woodrat populations are declining, possibly because of forest defoliation by gypsy moths and
infestation by parasites. Two species endemic to islands
in the Gulf of California—*N. anthonyi* of the Todos Santos
Islands and *N. bunkeri* of Isla Coronados—are probably
extinct owing to the depletion of native vegetation and
the introduction of domestic cats.

Woodrats belong to the subfamily Sigmodontinae of
the mouse family (Muridae) within the order Rodentia.

Fossils trace their history to the Late Miocene Epoch (11.2 million to 5.3 million years ago) of North America.

GROUPS THAT ARE NOT EXCLUSIVELY NOCTURNAL

Few rats move about during the day. Some groups, such as the dassie rats, are primarily diurnal and actually function quite well in the sunlight. In contrast, other groups, such as the cane rats, are occasionally active during the day. Blind mole rats, rodents known for their degenerative eyes and ears, are also considered here.

BLIND MOLE RATS

The eight living species of blind mole rats (subfamily Spalacinae) inhabit the eastern Mediterranean and Black Sea regions. Among the several rodents referred to as "mole rats," the blind mole rat is among the most molelike in form, having a furred, cylindrical body, short limbs, and protruding incisor teeth. The feet and claws are surprisingly small for such a highly specialized burrower. Blind mole rats appear eyeless and earless, as the functioning remnants of these structures are covered by fur and are therefore not visible. The tiny eyes are hidden beneath the skin, and the external ears are reduced to slight folds. Sensory bristles extending rearward from the flattened, padded nose toward the eyes give the head a keeled, wedgelike shape. Like the eyes and ears, the animal's minute stub of a tail is not visible externally.

Blind mole rats are medium-sized, weighing 100 to 570 grams (3.5 ounces to 1.3 pounds), with bodies about 13 to 35 cm (5.1 to 13.8 inches) long. The dense, soft fur may be pale to reddish brown or buff gray on the upperparts; underparts are grayish or buff brown. The front of the head is usually paler than the back and may exhibit white or yellow stripes, which can extend along the sides of the head or run down the middle of it from nose to forehead.

Territorial and solitary, the blind mole rat excavates a network of burrows by digging with its incisors, pushing the loosened soil beneath its belly with its forefeet, and then kicking the pile behind itself with its hind feet. When enough soil has accumulated, it turns around to pack some against the tunnel wall with its tough snout and uses its head to bulldoze any excess debris through the tunnel and onto the surface. Resulting mounds indicate tunnels 10 to 25 cm (3.9 to 9.8 inches) below ground in which the rodent searches for food. Their diet consists primarily of roots, tubers, and bulbs, but occasionally the animal emerges during the night to forage for seeds and green plant parts. Within the tunnels, vertical passageways connect the shallow burrows to deeper corridors where separate chambers for nesting, food storage, and excreta are constructed. During the wet autumn and winter, females build large mounds containing chambers where mating occurs and the young are reared. Gestation takes about a month, and litter size is from one to five.

Blind mole rats live in southeastern Europe, Turkey, the Middle East, and eastern North Africa near the shores of the Mediterranean Sea. Some species also range eastward to the Caspian Sea. Found at elevations from plains below sea level to high mountain clearings, these rodents prefer sandy or loamy soils of steppes, hillsides, dry brush country, woodlands, meadows, pastures, orchards, and cultivated fields in areas that receive at least 10 cm (3.9 inches) of annual rainfall. They avoid sandy or hard clay deserts.

There are two genera of blind mole rats: lesser, or Mediterranean, blind mole rats (three species in the genus *Nannospalax*) and greater, or Ukrainian, blind mole rats (five species in the genus *Spalax*). Together these genera constitute the subfamily Spalacinae of the mouse family (Muridae) within the order Rodentia. The African mole rats (genus *Tachyorytes*) and Central Asian mole rats are also members of the family Muridae but are not closely related, as they belong to different subfamilies. The evolutionary history of blind mole rats in the Mediterranean region is represented by fossils extending back 17 million to 19 million years to the Early Miocene Epoch (23.8 million to 16.4 million years ago).

Cane Rats

There are two species of cane rats (genus *Thryonomys*). Both of these African rodent species are large and stocky. Weighing up to 7 kg (more than 15 pounds), cane rats can grow to a length of 61 cm (24 inches), not including the scantily haired tail, which measures up to 26 cm (10.2 inches). Cane rats have blunt muzzles and small ears, and their speckled brown fur is coarse and bristly.

The greater cane rat (*Thryonomys swinderianus*) and the lesser cane rat (*T. gregorianus*) both inhabit nonforested sub-Saharan Africa except for Namibia and most of South Africa and Botswana. The two species are found together in certain regions, but they occupy different habitats. The greater cane rat lives along rivers and lakes and in swamps, reedbeds, and tall, dense grass with thick canelike stems, whereas the lesser cane rat prefers grassy ground in moist savannas and tall grass on rocky hillsides.

Cane rats are swift and agile on land and swim very well. Though primarily nocturnal, they are occasionally active during the day. Depending on the season, greater cane rats are solitary or communal. Lesser cane rats live in small family groups, usually denning in thick vegetation, although termite mounds and the abandoned burrows of aardvarks or porcupines are also used. Litters of one to eight well-developed young are born once or twice per year. Their diet consists of grass, other plants, and sometimes bark and fruits. Cane rats also eat crops and can become serious pests in regions where corn (maize), sugarcane, pineapples, cassava, and eggplant are cultivated. On the other hand, these large rodents provide a significant source of protein for Africans and are intensively hunted throughout their range.

Cane rats are the only living members of the family Thryonomyidae, and they have no close surviving relatives. The evolutionary history of *Thryonomys* dates back 2 million to 4 million years in Africa. However, fossils of extinct genera in the family Thryonomyidae have been found in Africa, the Mediterranean region, and Asia, and some of these remains date to the Late Eocene Epoch (37 million to 33.7 million years ago).

Cotton Rats

Cotton rats (genus *Sigmodon*) are terrestrial rodents found from the southern United States to northern South America. Cotton rats are stout-bodied with small ears, and their coarse, grizzled coats range from grayish brown to dark brown mixed with buff. All 10 species live in natural grassland habitats ranging from coastal marshes to mountain meadows. They also inhabit cultivated fields where grass or crops are sufficiently tall and dense to afford protection from predators. Active day and night, cotton rats use extensive surface trails through the grass that connect their fibrous nests, which they construct at the base of shrubs or in the burrows of other animals. Eating mostly plant materials, they can become serious agricultural pests, especially in plantations of sugarcane and vegetable crops.

Hispid cotton rat (Sigmodon hispidus). James Gathany/Centers for Disease Control and Prevention (CDC)

The hispid cotton rat (*S. hispidus*) has the most extensive distribution, extending from the southern United States to northern South America, and the natural history of this species has been the most intensely studied. It is large, weighing up to 225 grams (7.9 ounces), with a body up to 20 cm (nearly 8 inches) long and a tail up to 13 cm (about 5 inches) long. Although grasses and forbs are their primary diet, hispid cotton rats eat insects on a seasonal basis, crayfish and fiddler crabs in coastal marshes, and sometimes eggs and chicks of the bobwhite quail. Hispid cotton rats outnumber most other small mammals in grassland and agricultural areas of the southern United States. They are prolific, producing several litters of 4 to 8 young per year, although litters of 1 to 15 have been recorded.

In the United States, the hispid cotton rat is found from Florida and Virginia westward to New Mexico and Arizona. Its range expanded after European settlement, and in some of these areas populations of cotton rats have replaced those of the native prairie vole (*Microtus ochrogaster*). These two rodents are similar in both appearance and behaviour, the cotton rat being the prairie vole's larger-bodied ecological equivalent. Indeed, the meadow vole (*M. pennsylvanicus*), ranging from Alaska to the Eastern Seaboard, is also prolific and is the most abundant mammal in grassland and agricultural habitats north of the hispid cotton rat's range. Therefore, at northern latitudes the meadow vole is the ecological counterpart of the hispid cotton rat.

Cotton rats belong to the subfamily Sigmodontinae of the mouse and rat family, Muridae, within the order Rodentia.

DASSIE RATS

Dassie rats (*Petromus typicus*) are medium-sized rodents that have adapted to life among rocky outcrops in the desert hills and plateaus of southwestern Africa. The dassie rat weighs 170 to 300 grams (6 to 11 ounces) and has a squirrel-like body 14 to 21 cm (5.5 to 8.3 inches) long; its hairy tail is 12 to 17 cm (4.7 to 6.7 inches) long. The soft, silky fur ranges from pale gray to dark chocolate brown, although some populations have black coats. The dassie rat has a broad, flattened head and extremely flexible ribs and is thereby able to flatten itself against rocks and squeeze into tight places.

Active during the day, dassie rats move alone or in pairs and sun themselves when not foraging on grasses, flowers, leaves, and fruit. Among rodents, they are unique in regurgitating food into the mouth, chewing it again, and reswallowing, a behaviour found elsewhere only among artiodactyls such as cattle. Dassie rats are swift runners and agile jumpers in their rocky habitat, but they are also adept at climbing shrubs and trees to harvest leaves. They breed once a year in summer, bearing one or two well-developed young per litter.

Petromus typicus is the only living member of the family Petromuridae; the genus has also been called *Petromys* and the family Petromyidae. Both spellings of the name mean "rock mouse" in Greek. The dassie rat, however, is neither a rat nor a mouse (family Muridae); it is instead classified in the suborder Hystricognatha within the order Rodentia. The dassie rat's closest living relatives are the two species of cane rats (family Thyronomyidae). Dassie and cane rats are actually relict species, living remnants of an extinct lineage encompassing 17 genera from four or five families that lived in Africa as early as 35 million years ago during the Late Eocene Epoch.

SHREW RATS

Shrew rats belong to the subfamily of Old World rats and mice (Murinae) within the family Muridae of the order Rodentia. All 24 species are carnivorous ground dwellers. They are found only on the tropical islands of Sulawesi (Celebes), the Philippines, and New Guinea. Eighteen species live exclusively at high elevations in cool, wet mossy forests; the other six inhabit lowland and foothill rainforests.

These shrewlike mammals have small eyes, long whiskers, wide front feet, and narrow hindfeet with hairless soles. Other characteristics vary depending on the species: the body may be slender or chunky, the ears small or large; the tail may be shorter or longer than the body. The head and muzzle of several species are long and narrow, but among others the head is broad and the muzzle short. Nocturnal shrew rats have gray fur, but diurnal species are reddish brown to almost black. The Philippine striped rats (genus *Chrotomys*) and the blazed Luzon shrew rat (*Celaenomys silaceus*) have a stripe running down the back. Fur is generally short, dense, and soft. Its texture is either velvety or woolly, although the prickly coat of the Sulawesi spiny rat (*Echiothrix leucura*) is a striking exception. The Sulawesi spiny rat is the largest shrew rat, measuring 20 to 23 cm (7.9 to 9.1 inches), not including its slightly longer tail; it weighs 220 to 310 grams (about 8 to 11 ounces). Shrew rats of New Guinea are all very small—the groove-toothed shrew mouse (*Microhydromys richardsoni*) weighs only 9 to 12 grams (0.42 ounce) and has a body 8 to 9 cm (3.1 to 3.5 inches) long and an equally long tail.

Shrew rats poke their noses through wet leaf litter and moss to locate their food; those species with long front claws dig deeper into the ground cover and moist underlying soil. On Sulawesi and in the Philippines, large shrew rats share habitat with small white-toothed shrews; the shrew rats eat mostly earthworms, whereas the shrews consume insects. In New Guinea there are no shrews, but shrew rats are their ecological counterparts, primarily eating insects and other invertebrates. In the mountain forests of Sulawesi, some shrew rats are their own counterparts within the same habitat. Greater Sulawesian shrew rats (genus *Tateomys*) forage for earthworms at night, and the lesser Sulawesian shrew rat (*Melasmothrix naso*) exploits the same resource during the day.

WATER RATS

Water rats are amphibious and carnivorous rodents. Each of the 18 species included in this group exhibits many adaptations associated with hunting in water for food and burrowing along streams, rivers, and lakes. The eyes are small, the nostrils can be closed to keep water out, and the external portion of the ears is either small and furry or absent. Highly sensitive whiskers are abundant on the fleshy blunt muzzle. The long thick fur is gray or brown, dense and woolly, and water-repellent. The tail is usually densely haired, and in some species the hairs form a keel along the underside. The rats' long, wide hindfeet are fringed with stiff hairs and have bald soles with conspicuous webbing between the digits.

One of the smallest species is a South American fish-eating rat (*Neusticomys monticolus*) with a body length of 10 to 12 cm (4 to nearly 5 inches) and a tail of about the same length. The golden-bellied water rat (*Hydromys chrysogaster*) of Australia and New Guinea is the largest, with a body 20 to 39 cm (nearly 8 to about 15 inches) long and a slightly shorter tail (20 to 33 cm [nearly 8 to about 13 inches]). Living by freshwater lakes, estuaries, and rivers and in coastal mangrove swamps, the golden-bellied water rat is tolerant of heavily polluted aquatic habitats. Its prey includes a variety of invertebrates, such as large aquatic insects, snails, mussels, crabs, and crayfish. Vertebrates taken include fish, frogs, turtles, young and adult birds, bird eggs, bats, and mice. The other 17 species typically require clear, unpolluted freshwater streams. The animals' diet consists primarily of a variety of aquatic insects, but they also eat crustaceans and occasionally small fish. All water rats locate prey underwater by touch with their sensitive whiskers. Most are adept swimmers and aggressive underwater predators, but the African water rat (*Colomys goslingi*) wades through shallow water or sits at the water's edge with its muzzle submerged; it is reported to eat some terrestrial insects and snails. Although most water rats are nocturnal, some species are active during the day.

Water rats of the genus *Hydromys* live in the mountains and coastal lowlands of Australia, New Guinea, and some nearby islands. The earless water rat (*Crossomys moncktoni*) inhabits mountains of eastern New Guinea, where it prefers cold, fast-flowing streams bordered by tropical forest or grass. The African water rat is also found along streams bordered by tropical forest. The 11 water rats of the Western Hemisphere are found from southern Mexico into South America, where they typically live along streams in rainforests from sea level upward to mountain pastures above the tree line.

Although all water rats are members of the mouse family (Muridae), they belong to two different subfamilies. The genera *Hydromys*, *Crossomys*, and *Colomys* are classified in the subfamily Murinae (Old World mice and rats), whereas the American species are members of the subfamily Sigmodontinae (New World mice and rats). No water rats exist in the Asian tropics or at nontropical latitudes. Instead, carnivorous amphibious shrews and moles occupy the water rat's ecological niche. The European water voles (genus *Arvicola*) are sometimes called water rats.

CHAPTER 3
MICE AND SIMILAR FORMS

*M*ouse is the common name generally but imprecisely applied to rodents found throughout the world with bodies less than about 12 cm (5 inches) long. In a scientific context, *mouse* refers to any of the 38 species in the genus *Mus*, which is the Latin word for mouse. The house mouse (*Mus musculus*), native to Central Asia, has established itself with human populations in many other parts of the world.

All rodents with a mouselike or ratlike body, regardless of body size or diagnostic traits, were described as species of *Mus* between 1758 and the late 1800s. Subsequent study shifted most of those species into many different groups, leaving *Mus* as a smaller, clearly defined genus with a particular combination of traits. Within the genus there are four distinctive groups: spiny mice (subgenus *Pyromys*),

The house mouse (Mus musculus) *is a well-known species.* Encyclopædia Britannica, Inc.

shrew-mice (subgenus *Coelomys*), rice field mice and house mice (subgenus *Mus*), and African mice (subgenus *Nannomys*).

GENERAL FEATURES

Mice have slender bodies, blunt or tapered muzzles, scantily haired, prominent ears, narrow hind feet with bald soles, and sharp, small claws. The thinly furred tail appears hairless; it may be about as long as the head and body, or it can be much shorter. One of the largest is the flat-haired mouse (*M. platythrix*) of peninsular India, weighing about 18 grams (0.6 ounce), with a body 10 to 12 cm (4 to 4.7 inches) long and a shorter tail (7 to 8 cm [2.8 to 3.1 inches]). The smallest is probably the pygmy mouse (*M. minutoides*) of sub-Saharan Africa, weighing 3 to 12 grams (0.11 to 0.42 ounce), with a body 6 to 8 cm (2.3 to 3.1 inches) long and a short tail of 3 to 6 cm (1.2 to 2.3 inches).

There is considerable variation in fur texture and colour among the species of *Mus*. At one extreme are the spiny-furred species in the subgenus *Pyromys*, whose upperparts and undersides are covered with flat, channeled spines nestled in soft underfur (juveniles are not spiny). At the other extreme are the shrew-mice from Sumatra (*M. crociduroides*) and Java (*M. vulcani*), whose soft, short, and dense coat appears woolly or velvety. All the other species have a soft or slightly coarse, moderately thick coat with short or long hairs. A colour combination common to many mice is gray to brown upperparts, white underparts, white feet, and a tail that is dark above and white below. Variations of this pattern include upperparts of buff, bluish gray, blackish gray, reddish brown, or chocolate brown, with underparts ranging from white to various shades of gray, sometimes tinged with silver or buff. The feet may be white or the same colour as the upperparts, and the tail may be bicoloured or uniformly dark gray to dark brown.

NATURAL HISTORY

Mice in their natural habitats are primarily nocturnal, although some will occasionally forage during the day. They are ground dwellers, although some species are also agile climbers and leapers as well as capable swimmers. A few are specialized burrowers rarely seen above ground. Most species, especially those living in savannas and grasslands, excavate burrows and chambers in which they build globular nests of dry vegetation. In an intact ecosystem, species of *Mus*, along with other small-bodied rodents, are preyed upon, sometimes to an appreciable degree, by reptiles, mammals, and birds (especially owls).

The simple but effective excavation technique of mice is exemplified by the Ryukyu mouse (*M. caroli*). This mouse loosens soil with its incisor teeth, carrying a load of debris in its mouth and piling it outside the burrow entrance or sometimes stacking loose soil inside the burrow and then pushing the pile out with its hind feet. In the diked rice fields of Thailand, small piles of soil below holes in the dike signal the presence of Ryukyu mice. Each hole is the opening to a tunnel extending upward to a nest chamber above water level, then to another opening on the other side of the dike. Forest species may also burrow, but most of them construct nests in rock crevices or beneath rotting tree trunks and brush piles on the forest floor. The gray-bellied pygmy mouse (*M. triton*) of sub-Saharan Africa, for example, apparently does not burrow but uses pathways made by larger rodents.

Diet varies among species. Outdoors the house mouse consumes seeds and insects; indoors it eats nearly anything digestible. Most other species eat a combination of plant parts (especially seeds), insects, and other invertebrates. Stomachs of gray-bellied pygmy mice caught in East Africa, for example, contained plant parts, pieces of bark, insects (mostly adult beetles), and worms.

Depending upon the species and geographic region, mice may breed throughout the year or only during the wet seasons in southern latitudes and from spring to fall in northern latitudes. Except for the house mouse, which can produce up to 14 litters per year (1 to 12 offspring per litter), there is little information about the reproductive biology of most species. In the deserts of India, the little Indian field mouse (*M. booduga*) bears from 1 to 13 young per litter and breeds throughout the year. In Southeast Asia, the fawn-coloured mouse (*M. cervicolor*) has been reported to produce litters of two to six young in July and December. In East Africa, the pygmy mouse breeds during the wet seasons from April to June and September to December and bear litters of two to eight young.

GEOGRAPHIC DISTRIBUTION AND HABITAT

All species of *Mus* are native to Eurasia and Africa, where they range from lowlands to mountaintops. The five species in the subgenus *Pyromys* are found in Sri Lanka, India, and mainland Southeast Asia. Much of their range originally consisted of open grasslands or grassy patches in forests. Shortridge's mouse (*M. shortridgei*), for example, has been found living in tall grasses and pygmy bamboo growing among teak forests in Thailand.

The five species in the subgenus *Coelomys* are restricted to tropical evergreen lowland and mountain forests of Sri Lanka, southern India, mainland Southeast Asia, Sumatra, and Java. Beneath the forest understory, they live in moist or cool environments, often near streams and other water sources, or in wet, mossy habitats at high elevations. Little is known about their behaviour or ecology. They have tapered, shrewlike muzzles and small eyes. The dark brown fur is woolly or velvety in three of the species and somewhat spiny in the other two. Their diet probably consists mostly of invertebrates, which they locate by poking their noses through moist leaf litter and moss covering the forest floor.

The nine members of the subgenus *Mus* are found throughout Eurasia and North Africa in a variety of habitats: scantily vegetated deserts, steppes, rocky slopes, open grasslands and grassy patches in tropical deciduous forests, fallow fields and croplands at northern latitudes, and rice fields in the Asian tropics. Four of these species, including the house mouse, have dispersed beyond their natural ranges as a result of human settlement. The earth-coloured mouse (*M. terricolor*) is native to peninsular India, Nepal, and Pakistan, but it has been introduced into northern Sumatra. The fawn-coloured mouse has a natural distribution throughout mainland Southeast Asia and southern China but also inhabits rice fields on Sumatra and Java, where it was likely introduced. The Ryukyu mouse ranges throughout Southeast Asia, including Taiwan and the Ryukyu Islands, where it lives in rice fields and other grassy agricultural land; humans apparently introduced this species into the Malay Peninsula, Sumatra, Java, and east of the continental margin on Flores Island, where it inhabits rice fields.

Some species are apparently restricted to particular habitats, such as the gray-bellied pygmy mouse (*M. triton*), which lives only in grassland, heath, and wet scrub, but others are more adaptable. Habitats of the pygmy mouse, for example, include open sandy ground, savannas, forests, and sometimes houses. This subgenus contains the most efficient burrowers: Thomas's pygmy mouse (*M. sorella*) and its relatives have protruding upper incisors, longer claws than most species of *Mus*, and shorter tails relative to body length. They are rarely seen and are caught only by being dug out of their burrows.

The 19 species of subgenus *Nannomys* live throughout sub-Saharan Africa in many different habitats: sandy and stony deserts, open grasslands, heath, scrub, dry and wet savannas, lowland to montane tropical forests, swamp margins, and cultivated areas.

EVOLUTIONARY HISTORY

Species of *Mus* belong to the subfamily of Old World rats and mice (Murinae) in the family Muridae within the order Rodentia. Their closest living relative is the stripe-backed mouse (*Muriculus imberbis*) endemic to the mountains of Ethiopia. The evolutionary history of *Mus* extends 6 million years to the late Miocene Epoch in Asia, 3 million to 4 million years to the Pliocene Epoch in Africa and Europe, and 11,700 to 2.6 million years to the Pleistocene Epoch in the Mediterranean region. Based upon study of living and fossil species, researchers speculate that *Mus* originated in central Asia more than 11 million years ago, evolved into the many fossil and living Asian species, entered Africa around 5 million years ago (where it formed the ancestral stock of fossil and living *Nannomys* species), and finally reached Europe and the Mediterranean somewhat later.

TYPES OF MICE

Like rats, mice are overwhelmingly nocturnal. Nocturnal species avoid the heat of the day and are less conspicuous to potential predators. Mice that are at least partially diurnal, however, must contend with these threats. Several mouse groups are classified by their periods of activity below.

Predominantly Nocturnal Groups

Nocturnal mouse groups are numerous. Asian tree mice rest in the trees during the day, whereas jerboas, which inhabit arid and semiarid regions in Eurasia and Africa, hide in their burrows to escape the heat. Other nocturnal groups include the jumping mice, pocket mice, and wood mice.

Asian Tree Mice

Asian tree mice (subfamily Platacanthomyinae) consist of three species of small rodents found only in a few tropical forests of India and continental Southeast Asia.

The Malabar spiny tree mouse (*Platacanthomys lasiurus*) lives only in the old-growth rainforests of southwestern India. Nocturnal and arboreal, it builds nests in tree cavities and eats fruits and nuts. The animal is named for its flat, grooved spines and bristles, which are tipped with white and protrude from a dark brown coat of thin, soft underfur. The underside is less spiny and is pale in colour. Near the base of the tail, the hairs are short, but they become progressively longer toward the bushy white tip, which makes the tail resemble a bottlebrush. This slender rodent measures about 12 to 14 cm (4.5 to 5.5 inches), not including the slightly shorter tail. The feet end in sharp, curved claws except for the short first toe, which bears a nail. The prominent ears are nearly bald and the whiskers extremely long.

The other two Asian tree mice are called blind tree mice (genus *Typhlomys*): the Chinese blind tree mouse (*T. cinereus*) and the Chapa blind tree mouse (*T. chapensis*). They are probably nocturnal and arboreal, inhabiting mountain forests of southern China and northern Vietnam, respectively. Aside from their physical traits, little is known of these rodents. They resemble the Malabar mouse in body form, but their fur is spineless, and their tails are not nearly as bushy. The feet bear a claw instead of a nail on the first hind toe. The blind tree mice are smaller, with a body length of 7 to 10 cm (2.8 to 3.9 inches), but the tail is longer than the head and body (9 to 14 cm [3.5 to 5.5 inches]). The short, soft, dense fur is dark gray with lighter underparts.

Originally considered to be dormice (family Myoxidae), Asian tree mice are now classified as the only members of subfamily Platacanthomyinae of the "true" mouse and rat family (Muridae). Their closest living relatives are unknown, but fossils representing extinct species of both Asian tree mouse genera have been found in sediments from the Late Miocene Epoch (11.2 million to 5.3 million years ago) in southern China. Fossils of a related genus (*Neocometes*) from Europe and Asia are even older; thus, the living species are remnants of a past Eurasian distribution.

BIRCH MICE

Birch mice (genus *Sicista*) are small, long-tailed, mouselike rodents. The 13 known species live in the northern forests, thickets, and subalpine meadows and steppes of Europe and Asia. Their bodies are 5 to 10 cm (2 to 4 inches) long, excluding the semi-prehensile tail that is longer than the head and body. Birch mice are brown or yellowish brown with slightly paler underparts, and some species have a dark stripe extending over the head and back. They eat both plant material and insects, live in burrows, and hibernate underground from fall into spring. All travel on the ground by leaping, but they are also good climbers, using their tails as additional support.

For many years only six species of birch mouse were recognized; beginning in the 1970s, however, intensive study by Russian and Chinese scientists of populations in eastern Europe, Central Asia, and China revealed seven additional species. Birch mice are not "true mice" (family Muridae);

they belong to a different family (Dipodidae) that includes the jumping mice of China and North America. Birch mice and jumping mice belong to different subfamilies within the family Dipodidae of the order Rodentia.

Fossils have also provided knowledge about the species diversity and geographic distribution of birch mice. Relatives of birch mice lived in North America from the Middle Miocene to the Early Pleistocene epoch. The evolutionary history of birch mice apparently began in Eurasia, where its closest relatives are represented by fossils of the extinct genera *Plesiosminthus* and *Heterosminthus* from 25-million to 28-million-year-old sediments of the Oligocene Epoch. *Sicista* fossils have been found in Asia from as far back as the late Miocene (11.6 to 5.3 million years ago) and in Europe in the late Pliocene (3.6 to 2.6 million years ago).

Grasshopper Mice

Three species of grasshopper mice (genus *Onychomys*) exist. Terrestrial, nocturnal, insectivorous, and carnivorous, grasshopper mice are physiologically adapted to semiarid and arid habitats in the open country of western North America. The northern grasshopper mouse (*Onychomys leucogaster*) lives in grassland and shrub steppes from central Canada southward through the Great Plains and Great Basin to northern Mexico. The southern grasshopper mouse (*O. torridus*) is found from southern California, Nevada, and Utah southward to northeastern Mexico. Mearns' grasshopper mouse (*O. arenicola*) ranges from the southwestern United States to central Mexico. The last two species prefer warm, very arid, scrubby desert habitats. All are stout bodied, weighing up to 49 grams (1.7 ounces) and having a body length up to 13 cm (just over 5 inches) and a much shorter tail of up to 6 cm (2.4 inches). The coat is silky and dense; the underparts are white;

and the upperparts range from grayish to reddish brown, depending upon the species.

Often living in the burrows of prairie dogs, kangaroo rats, and pocket mice, grasshopper mice also construct their own burrows for nesting and food storage. They mostly eat insects, especially grasshoppers, beetles, crickets, and scorpions, but also stalk, kill, and eat other small rodents such as kangaroo rats, white-footed mice, and voles. Seeds constitute only a small part of their diet. Because their population densities are low and because they are highly aggressive, strongly territorial, and voracious, grasshopper mice are regarded as small analogues of larger mammalian carnivores. These mice even communicate over long distances with a pure-tone howl that is audible to humans—like a miniature version of a coyote howl.

The three living *Onychomys* species belong to the subfamily Sigmodontinae of the "true" mouse family, Muridae, within the order Rodentia. Today's *Onychomys* species are related to grasshopper mice represented by four-million to five-million-year-old fossils that extend the evolutionary history of the genus back to the Early Pliocene Epoch (5.3 million to 3.6 million years ago) in North America.

HOUSE MICE

House mice (*Mus musculus*) are rodents native to Eurasia but were introduced worldwide through their association with humans. Highly adaptive, the house mouse has both behavioral and physiological traits that allow it to thrive wherever humans do, such as the ability to survive in buildings and aboard ships, a tendency to move into agricultural fields and leave when the habitat changes, and a rapid rate of reproduction.

The house mouse has thin whiskers, narrow hind feet, and short, sharp claws; its long, slender, scantily haired tail and prominent, thinly furred ears appear naked, but on the rest of the body the fur is short and soft. Domesticated laboratory strains may be white (true albinos), black, patterned with black and white, or blond, whereas native populations have tawny-brown upperparts and white bellies with shorter, bicoloured tails. Introduced feral populations, on the other hand, have dark, grayish brown upperparts paling to gray on the sides; underparts are similar to the sides and sometimes tinged with buff, and the tail is uniformly dark gray. The animal has a distinctive strong, musky odour. Generally weighing 12 to 30 grams (0.4 to 1.1 ounces), the house mouse has a small, slender body 6 to 11 cm (2.4 to 4.3 inches) long, and its tail length equals its body length. All these dimensions, however, can vary among different populations around the world.

House mice are primarily nocturnal and terrestrial. Nervously active, they are agile climbers and jumpers and are also good swimmers. Outdoors, they excavate burrows in which to build nests of dry grass, but they will also den among rocks and crevices. House mice living

outdoors eat insects and seeds, including grains, which makes them pests in some areas. Indoor house mice are also considered pests; essentially omnivorous, they construct nests in any protected place and can contaminate food and damage property. Indoor house mice breed throughout the year, but outdoor populations at temperate latitudes breed only

House mouse (Mus musculus). Ingmar Holmasen

from early spring until late fall. Gestation lasts 19 to 21 days, and each female of these prolific rodents can produce up to 14 litters per year (5 to 10 is usual); 5 or 6 young per litter is normal, although litters of up to 12 are sometimes produced. Life span can be as long as three years in laboratory mice but is considerably shorter among free-living mice.

Eurasia is the modern natural range of house mice, but researchers speculate that this is the result of migration from a likely habitat of origin in the grasslands of the northern Indian subcontinent. In tropical Asia, where their natural habitats are occupied by other, closely related species of *Mus*, house mice live only in buildings. Populations at temperate latitudes, however, can inhabit buildings (either seasonally or throughout the year) or live outside in grasslands, fallow fields, croplands, grassy coastal dunes, or shrubby deserts. When fields are plowed or crops harvested, these mice move into other fields or houses but not into forests.

Western Europe is the primary source of house mice introduced into the United States, but a small population in southern California came from Asia. Humans eventually learned to domesticate and breed laboratory mice, which are an inbred genetic mosaic of European, Japanese, and Chinese stocks used in biomedical and genetic research.

House mice are one of 38 species in the genus *Mus*, a member of the subfamily Murinae in the mouse family Muridae within the order Rodentia.

Jerboas

Jerboas constitute a group of 33 species of long-tailed leaping rodents well adapted to the deserts and steppes of eastern Europe, Asia, and northern Africa. Jerboas are mouselike, with bodies ranging from 5 to 15 cm (2 to 5.9 inches) in length and long tails of 7 to 25 cm (2.8 to 9.8

inches). Certain traits are highly variable between species, particularly the size of the ears, which range from small and round to slender and rabbitlike or remarkably large and broad. Hind toes number from three to five, but all species have short forelegs and extremely long hind legs. The tail is often tufted. Jerboas' dense fur is either silky or velvety in texture and light in colour, usually matching the ground of the animal's habitat.

Jerboas leap up to 3 metres (10 feet) at a bound when alarmed or traveling swiftly, but when moving slowly they walk on their hind legs and sometimes hop by using all four limbs. The long tail props up the animal when it stands and is used for balance when it springs away. By day jerboas rest in burrows; they emerge at night to forage for seeds, succulent parts of plants, and insects. Some species plug their burrow entrances with soil to retain moisture and keep hot air out. Most are dormant during winter. Although jerboas drink water in captivity, in natural habitats they obtain it from food.

The 33 jerboa species are taxonomically diverse, with members belonging to five different subfamilies within the family Dipodidae, which also includes birch mice and jumping mice. Fossil evidence dates the jerboas' evolutionary history back to the Middle Miocene Epoch (16.4 million to 11.2 million years ago) in North Africa and Asia.

Jumping Mice

There are five living species of jumping mice (subfamily Zapodinae). They are small leaping rodents found in North America and China. Jumping mice weigh from 13 to 26 grams (0.5 to 0.9 ounce) and are 8 to 11 cm (3.1 to 4.3 inches) long, not including the scantily haired tail, which is longer than the body. Their glossy fur is soft or slightly coarse; coloration is divided into three parts: brown on top from nose to rump, grayish to rust-coloured on the sides,

Meadow jumping mouse (Zapus hudsonius). Stephen Collins/Photo Researchers

and white on the underparts. The tail is brown above and white below.

Jumping mice normally run on all four legs or bounce along in a series of short hops, but when alarmed they leap powerfully yet erratically up to 4 metres (13 feet), using their disproportionately long hind legs. They are balanced by the slender tail.

Generally terrestrial, these rodents are also agile shrub climbers and excellent swimmers. Their spherical nests are constructed of vegetation and are found in abandoned burrows of other animals, on the ground beneath logs or heavy brush, and sometimes in low shrubs and trees. Jumping mice eat a varied diet of fungi, fruit, seeds, invertebrates, and occasionally mollusks and small fish. During the winter they retreat underground to hibernate.

North American jumping mice, though common in some areas, are rarely seen because they are completely nocturnal. The woodland jumping mouse (*Napaeozapus insignis*) lives in moist forests of eastern North America. The meadow, Pacific, and western jumping mice (*Zapus hudsonius*, *Z. trinotatus*, and *Z. princeps*, respectively) range over much of North America, in grasslands as well as riverine and wet meadow habitats of cool and moist forests. The only species found outside North America is the Sichuan jumping mouse (*Eozapus setchuanus*), which inhabits cool and wet mountain forests of southern China. It is sometimes incorrectly included in the genus *Zapus*. Very little is known about its natural history.

Jumping mice constitute the subfamily Zapodinae. Along with birch mice and the more distantly related jerboas, jumping mice are classified in the family Dipodidae rather than with the "true" mice (family Muridae). Fossils of four extinct genera provide evolutionary history of jumping mice from the Middle Miocene Epoch (16.4 million to 11.2 million years ago) in North America and the Late Miocene Epoch (11.2 million to 5.3 million years ago) in Eurasia.

KANGAROO MICE

Kangaroo mice (genus *Microdipodops*) are leaping bipedal rodents found only in certain deserts of the western United States. Each of the two known species possesses large ears and a large head with fur-lined external cheek pouches. The forelimbs are short, but the hind limbs and feet are long. Stiff hairs fringe the hind feet, and the soles are densely furred. The soft, silky coat is long and lax.

The dark kangaroo mouse (*Microdipodops megacephalus*) has buff or brownish upperparts tinted with black and has gray or whitish underparts with a black-tipped tail, whereas the upperparts and entire tail of the pale kangaroo mouse

(*M. pallidus*) are creamy buff and the underparts are white. Kangaroo mice weigh 10 to 17 grams (0.4 to 0.6 ounce) and have a body length of 7 to 8 cm (about 3 inches) and a tail 6 to 10 cm (2.4 to 3.9 inches) long. The tail is used for balance as the mouse moves across the ground via leaps and bounds. The middle of the tail bulges slightly owing to its deposit of stored fat, a unique feature of small mammals native to North America. The deposit enlarges during the summer and is used as an energy source during hibernation.

Kangaroo mice live in valley bottoms and alluvial fans of the Great Basin, where stabilized dunes of fine wind-blown sand and other sandy soils are common. Where ranges of the two species overlap in Nevada, the dark kangaroo mouse prefers fine gravelly soil. The simple burrows of kangaroo mice are usually excavated with the entrance near a shrub. When foraging on open ground away from any shrub canopy, they carry food in their cheek pouches to the burrow for storage. The mice are active only during the cool desert nights, and they further reduce their water needs by producing concentrated urine and dry feces. Kangaroo mice do not need to drink water; instead, they obtain what they require from a diet of seeds and the occasional insect. Winter is cold and harsh in the high Great Basin, and kangaroo mice survive it by hibernating from about November until March. Breeding all summer, they can produce multiple litters of two to seven young apiece.

Kangaroo mice are thought of as smaller versions of kangaroo rats. They can be distinguished by the tail, which, unlike that of the larger kangaroo rats, is neither crested nor tufted. Both groups belong to the family Heteromyidae (Greek: "other mice," or "different mice") and are not classified with the "true" mice (family Muridae). Pocket mice are related to kangaroo mice and also belong to the family Heteromyidae, which is related to the pocket gopher family (Geomyidae) within the order Rodentia.

Pocket Mice

The 36 known species of pocket mice belong to the family Heteromyidae. Pocket mice occur in North and South America, and they are known by their fur-lined external cheek pouches that open alongside the mouth. The pouches are used for storing food, particularly seeds, as the animal forages.

Like "true" mice and rats (family Muridae), pocket mice travel on all four limbs along the ground, as opposed to hopping like their relative, the kangaroo mouse. Pocket mice are nocturnal and usually solitary. They eat seeds, succulent plant parts, and nuts, carrying food (mainly seeds) in their cheek pouches to hoard in burrows. Most are active all year, even some of those living at northern latitudes. Others remain in burrows during winter or on hot days in summer; they may become torpid but do not hibernate.

The nine species of silky pocket mice (genus *Perognathus*) are very small, weighing from 5 to 30 grams (0.2 to 1.1 ounces) with a body length of 6 to 9 cm (2.4 to 3.5 inches) and hairy tails 5 to 10 cm (2 to 3.9 inches) long. Silky pocket mice have soft fur ranging from yellowish to gray on the upperparts and white to buff on the underparts; soles of the hind feet are furry, but in all other pocket mice the soles are hairless.

The 15 species of coarse-haired pocket mice (genus *Chaetodipus*) are larger on average, weighing 15 to 47 grams (0.53 to 1.7 ounces) and having a body length of 8 to 13 cm (3.1 to 5.1 inches) and hairy, tufted tails as long as or much longer than the body (up to 15 cm [5.9 inches]). Coarse-haired pocket mice are similar in colour to silky pocket mice, but the fur is harsh and the rump has spiny bristles. Silky and coarse-haired pocket mice range from western Canada and the United States into southern Mexico, where they inhabit open desert country.

The five species of spiny pocket mice (genus *Liomys*) are found in extreme southern Texas, but they live mostly in Mexico southward to Panama in semiarid brushy and rocky habitats. These pocket mice weigh 34 to 50 grams (1.2 to 1.8 ounces) and have a body length of 10 to 14 cm (3.9 to 5.5 inches) and long tails of up to 16 cm (6.3 inches).

The seven species of forest spiny pocket mice (genus *Heteromys*) are the largest, weighing from 37 to 85 grams (1.3 to 3 ounces) and having 11- to 18-cm (4.3- to 7.1-inch) bodies and long scantily haired tails. Forest pocket mice range from southern Mexico to northern South America, where they live from sea level upward into mountains. All the spiny pocket mice have harsh fur made up of stiff, bristly hairs that may be gray, reddish brown, dark brown, or glossy black. In some species a rust-coloured strip separates upperparts and underparts.

Pocket mice are classified in the family Heteromyidae, meaning "different mouse," or "other mouse," in Greek. This family also includes kangaroo rats and kangaroo mice. Within Heteromyidae, the silky and coarse-haired pocket mice constitute the subfamily Perognathinae, and the spiny pocket mice constitute the subfamily Heteromyinae. Spiny pocket mice are more ratlike and probably bear a closer structural resemblance to the family's extinct fossil ancestors than do any other living members.

Wood Mice

Wood mice (genus *Apodemus*) make up about 20 species of small-bodied rodents, and they are distributed eastward from northern Europe to southern China and the Himalayas. Body size varies; different species weigh from 15 to 50 grams (0.5 to 1.8 ounces) and measure from 6 to 15 cm (2.4 to 5.9 inches) long excluding the tail, which is either about as long as the head and body or much shorter. Wood mice have soft fur that is yellowish brown or gray; the

Long-tailed field mouse (Apodemus sylvaticus). Stephen Dalton/EB Inc.

striped field mouse (*Apodemus agrarius*) has a narrow black stripe down its back.

Wood mice inhabit forests, grasslands, and cultivated fields. They generally live in burrows and build nests of grass and other plants, but during harsh seasons they will move into buildings. Their diet includes seeds, roots, fruit, and insects. Most wood mice are nocturnal and terrestrial; a few, including the striped field mouse, are active during the day, and some, particularly the Japanese wood mouse (*A. argenteus*), are agile climbers. The long-tailed field mouse (*A. sylvaticus*) is one of the most intensively studied species in the genus. In Europe it ranges north to Scandinavia and east to Ukraine. This wood mouse is also found in North Africa and on many islands. Once considered indigenous to Iceland, it was probably introduced by European settlers in the 10th and 11th centuries.

Apodemus species are classified in the subfamily Murinae of "true" mice (family Muridae) in the order Rodentia. Fossils representing 28 species document the past diversity of the genus, with the oldest dating from the Middle Miocene Epoch (16.4 million to 11.2 million years ago) in Europe. *Apodemus* and *Mus* (which includes the house mouse) are the only genera of the more than 125 within Murinae that span such a long geologic time period.

GROUPS THAT ARE NOT EXCLUSIVELY NOCTURNAL

Diurnal species include African spiny mice, dormice, and voles. Although several species in these groups prefer to be active at night, at least some individuals have been observed moving about during the day. Since mice are prey for raptors, reptiles, and other mammals, daytime activity is limited by the quality of vegetative cover.

AFRICAN SPINY MICE

African spiny mice (genus *Acomys*) constitute more than a dozen species of small- to medium-sized rodents characterized by the harsh, inflexible spiny hairs of their upperparts. African spiny mice have large eyes and ears and scaly, nearly bald tails that are shorter than or about as long as the body. The tail is brittle and breaks off readily either as a whole or in part. The golden spiny mouse (*Acomys russatus*), found from Egypt to Saudi Arabia, is one of the largest, with a body up to 25 cm (9.8 inches) long and a shorter tail of up to 7 cm (2.8 inches). The Cape spiny mouse (*A. subspinosus*) of South Africa is one of the smallest, with a body up to 10 cm (3.9 inches) long and a tail of less than 2 cm (0.8 inch). Depending upon the species, fur covering the upperparts may be gray, grayish yellow, brownish red, or reddish. Black (melanistic) individuals occur in populations of the golden spiny mouse and the Cairo spiny mouse (*A. cahirinus*).

African spiny mice are omnivorous, though plant materials form the bulk of their diet. In Egypt some Cairo spiny mice eat mostly dates, but others have been reported to consume the dried flesh and bone marrow of mummies in the tombs of Gebel Drunka, southwest of Asyut. All species are ground dwellers, and most are nocturnal, some being more active during early morning and evening. The golden spiny mouse is diurnal and occupies the same habitat as the Cairo spiny mouse, which is its nocturnal counterpart—the two species exploit the same food resources but at different times. Females of certain species will assist mothers during birth by biting the umbilical cord and licking and cleaning the newborn mice.

African spiny mice range through the northern, eastern, and southern regions of Africa eastward through southwestern Asia and southern Pakistan to the Indus River. They are also found in southern Turkey and on the islands of Cyprus and Crete. Living in rocky, partially vegetated deserts, savannas, and dry woodlands, they den in rock crevices, termite mounds, or other rodents' burrows. The Cairo spiny mouse has the most extensive distribution, extending from northern Africa to the Indus River; it lives near or with humans in some parts of its range. The most restricted is *A. cilicicus*, which is known only from a single locality in southern Turkey.

Different authorities classify African spiny mice into as few as 14 species and as many as 19. The genus was once grouped with other Old World rats and mice of the subfamily Murinae in the family Muridae, but analyses of dental and molecular data suggest that the African spiny mice form a distinctive and separate subfamily, Acomyinae. Other African rodents proved to be close relatives of African spiny mice and were also reclassified in this subfamily; these are Rudd's mouse (*Uranomys ruddi*), the Congo forest mouse (*Deomys ferrugineus*), and brush-furred rats (genus *Lophuromys*).

Fossils of extinct species trace the ancestry of African spiny mice to the Late Miocene Epoch (11.2 million to 5.3 million years ago) in Africa, where they probably lived in habitats not unlike the dry savannas in which existing species are found.

DEER MICE

Deer mice (genus *Peromyscus*) are small rodents found in a variety of habitats from Alaska and northern Canada southward to western Panama. The 53 species in this group have bulging eyes and large ears, weigh from 15 to 110 grams (0.5 to 3.9 ounces), and are 8 to 17 cm (3.1 to 6.7 inches) long. The tail may be shorter than the head and body or strikingly longer, depending on the species. All deer mice have soft fur, but colour varies both between and within species. The fur is nearly white in some populations of cotton mice (*Peromyscus gossypinus*) in the

Deer mouse (Peromyscus). Ken Brate—Photo Researchers/EB Inc.

southeastern United States, but it can range from gray through bright buff, brown, reddish brown, and to blackish in *P. melanurus*, which inhabits the mountain forests of southern Mexico. Species living in dark and wet forests tend to have dark coats, whereas those adapted to deserts and prairies are generally pale; nearly all have white feet.

Deer mice are nocturnal but are occasionally active in the early evening. They spend daylight hours in burrows or in trees, where they construct nests of plant material. Although terrestrial, they are agile climbers. Their diet includes everything from plant products and fungi to invertebrates and carrion.

P. maniculatus is sometimes called the white-footed mouse and has the most extensive geographic distribution of any North American rodent. Found from Canada to subtropical Mexico, it lives in a spectacular range of habitats between the Canadian tundra and the Sonoran Desert; it also lives in temperate and boreal forests, grasslands, and scrub formations. Females produce up to four litters per year after 21 to 27 days' gestation, and each litter usually contains three to five young (one to eight are extremes). The white-footed mouse breeds readily in laboratory settings, and across the United States it is used for studies involving genetics, evolution, physiology, and medicine. *P. maniculatus* is the primary host of hantavirus and one of the hosts of plague, and it is also one of several mammalian hosts that can transmit Lyme disease in the United States.

In the early 21st century, some evolutionary biologists asserted that the colour changes occurring in the fur of a population of *P. maniculatus* was one of the purest examples of natural selection. Research suggests that a gene associated with lighter-coloured fur, nicknamed *Agouti* by scientists, emerged naturally between 8,000 and 15,000 years ago in some deer mice that inhabited a unique sand dune environment in Nebraska, U.S.

LYME DISEASE

Lyme disease is a tick-borne bacterial disease that was first conclusively identified in 1975 and is named for the town in Connecticut, U.S., in which it was first observed. The disease has been identified in every region of the United States and in Europe, Asia, Africa, and Australia.

Lyme disease is caused by the spirochete (corkscrew-shaped bacterium) *Borrelia burgdorferi*. The spirochete is transmitted to the human bloodstream by the bite of various species of ticks. In the northeastern United States, the carrier tick is usually *Ixodes dammini;* in the West, *I. pacificus;* and in Europe, *I. ricinus*. Ticks pick up the spirochete by sucking the blood of deer or other infected animals. *I. dammini* mainly feeds on white-tailed deer and white-footed mice, especially in areas of tall grass, and is most active in summer. The larval and nymphal stages of this tick are more likely to bite humans than are the adult and are therefore more likely to cause human cases of the disease.

In humans the disease progresses in three stages. The first and mildest stage is characterized by a circular rash in a bull's-eye pattern that appears anywhere from a few days to a month after the tick bite (although it is important to note that not all of those infected develop the rash, and still others, who do, may not notice it). The rash is often accompanied by such flulike symptoms as headache, fatigue, chills, loss of appetite, fever, and aching joints or muscles. The majority of persons who contract Lyme disease experience only these first-stage symptoms and never become seriously ill. A minority, however, will go on to the second stage of the disease, which begins two weeks to three months after infection. This stage is indicated by arthritic pain that migrates from joint to joint and by disturbances of memory, vision, movement, or other neurological symptoms. The third stage of Lyme disease, which generally begins within two years of the bite, is marked by crippling arthritis and by neurological symptoms that resemble those of multiple sclerosis. Symptoms vary widely, however, and some persons experience facial paralysis, meningitis, memory loss, mood swings, and an inability to concentrate.

Because Lyme disease often mimics other disorders, its diagnosis is sometimes difficult, especially when there is no record of the distinctive rash. Early treatment of Lyme disease with antibiotics is important in order to prevent progression of the disease to a more serious stage. More powerful antibiotics are used in the latter case, though symptoms may recur periodically thereafter.

This mutation allowed some mice to better camouflage themselves against the sand-coloured background of the dunes, and it is thought that over thousands of generations the frequency of the *Agouti* gene increased in this population while the frequency of the gene associated with darker fur declined. Some scientists contend that the colour changes occurring in deer mice may serve as a more useful example of natural selection in action than the 19th-century colour change observed in peppered moths (*Biston betularia*) in England that was attributed to industrial melanism.

Deer mice belong to the subfamily Sigmodontinae of the mouse family (Muridae). Their closest living relatives are American harvest mice (genus *Reithrodontomys*).

DESERT DORMICE

The desert dormouse (*Selevinia betpakdalaensis*) is a rarely seen or captured small rodent of Central Asia. Weighing less than 28 grams (1 ounce), the desert dormouse has a stout rounded body 8 to 10 cm (3.1 to 3.9 inches) long and a slightly shorter fine-haired tail of 6 to 8 cm (2.4 to 3.1 inches). Its gray fur is long, soft, and dense, and its underside is white. The molt of this species is unique in that patches of both skin and hair are sloughed off and replaced by a dense new growth. Other rodents replace their hair during the molt but not the skin. The upper incisor teeth are large, but the cheek teeth are very small, barely jutting above the gums.

The desert dormouse is an endangered species that lives only in the clay and sandy deserts surrounding Lake Balkhash in southeastern Kazakhstan. The first scientific record of the species came from the Betpaqdala Desert west of the lake (hence the latter portion of the scientific name, *betpakdalaensis*). The species is patchily distributed among thickets of boyalych saltbush (*Salsola laricifolia*) and white wormwood (*Artemisia maritime*) growing on salty clay soils.

The desert dormouse has been observed during the day but is active primarily at night, when temperatures are cooler. It ambles along unless disturbed, at which time it proceeds with slow, short leaps; it also climbs well. Because the ecology of wild populations has not been studied, most information about the animal's habits comes from captive individuals. One individual dug a burrow only at low temperatures; at high temperatures it sheltered beneath a leaf or rock. Another animal became dormant at temperatures below 5 °C (41 °F). Dormancy may explain the animal's apparent scarcity during cold periods. Spiders and insects were eaten in captivity, and leaves of boyalych shrubs have been found in the stomachs of specimens caught in the wild. Females have been reported to contain six or eight embryos.

The researchers who originally described the species in 1939 named it Selevin's mouse, and they grouped it in the mouse and rat family, Muridae, of the order Rodentia. Later, the same researchers proposed classifying it as the sole member of its own family, allied with dormice (family Myoxidae). By 1947 detailed study had demonstrated that the desert dormouse was indeed a specialized species of dormouse. Thus, it is now included with three other dormouse genera in a subfamily (Leithiinae) of Myoxidae. A fossil from the Early Pliocene Epoch (5.3 million to 3.6 million years ago) in Poland represents an extinct species (genus *Proselevinia*) closely related to the living desert dormouse.

DORMICE

There are 27 known species of dormice (family Myoxidae). All are small-bodied rodents inhabiting Eurasian, Japanese, and African environments. The largest, weighing up to 180 grams (6.3 ounces), is the fat, or edible, dormouse (*Glis glis*) of Europe and the Middle East, with a body up to 19 cm

(7.5 inches) long and a shorter tail up to 15 cm (5.9 inches). One of the smallest is the Japanese dormouse of southern Japan (*Glirulus japonicus*), weighing up to 40 grams (1.4 ounces) and having a body that measures less than 8 cm (3.1 inches) long and a tail of up to 6 cm (2.4 inches). Dormice are small to medium-sized and have large eyes, rounded ears, short legs and digits, and hairy or bushy tails. Their gray to reddish fur is soft and dense; some species have a dark stripe along the back and dark facial markings.

Dormice are primarily nocturnal, but some are active during the day. Most species are arboreal and agile climbers, but some thrive in treeless, arid regions. Some are adept rock climbers, reportedly able to scale vertical rock faces and even walk upside down under rock ledges. Dormice construct globular nests in trees, bushes, rock crevices, and burrows and among tree roots; some also utilize abandoned bird or squirrel nests and, occasionally, active beehives. Their diet consists of fruit, nuts, insects, spiders, bird eggs and nestlings, and small rodents — even other dormice.

Dormice are found in Eurasia from western Europe to eastern China, in southern Japan, along the Mediterranean margin of North Africa, and throughout sub-Saharan

Edible dormouse (Glis glis). Schunemann/ Bavaria-Verlag

Africa. They live in a diverse variety of habitats from boreal and deciduous forests to orchards and tropical rainforests, through open country broken by scattered clusters of trees and shrubs to clay and sandy deserts and rocky, dry plateaus. Species living at temperate and boreal latitudes accumulate body fat in the fall and hibernate during much of the winter, rousing occasionally to eat food that they have stored. Tropical and desert species experience periods of torpor but not hibernation.

Dormice are not "true" mice (family Muridae); they are the only members of family Myoxidae, but their relationship to other rodents is not clear. Dormice have been allied with two different major groups: the squirrel-like rodents (suborder Sciuromorpha) and the mouselike rodents (suborder Myomorpha). In reality, the closest living relatives of dormice are unknown. The dormouse family has a long and diverse evolutionary history from the Early Eocene Epoch (54.8 million to 49 million years ago) in Europe and Asia and from the Middle Miocene Epoch (16.4 million to 11.2 million years ago) in Africa; this history produced today's living forms as well as numerous extinct species in 36 genera that are represented only by fossils.

HARVEST MICE

Harvest mice belong to either of two genera of small mice. The first, the American harvest mouse (*Reithrodontomys*), is native to North and South America, whereas the second, the Old World harvest mouse (*Micromys*), is native to Eurasia.

American Harvest Mice

The 20 species of American harvest mice are widespread, being found from southern Canada to northern South America at elevations ranging from below sea level to above the timberline in the northern Andes Mountains. They live in prairies, grassy fields with shrubs or trees, meadows, temperate and tropical forests, and cultivated fields. One, the salt-marsh harvest mouse (*R. raviventris*), lives only in the tidal salt marshes surrounding San Francisco Bay in California and is listed as an endangered species under federal and state laws. American harvest mice are nocturnal and are active all year. Although terrestrial, they are excellent climbers and build globular nests of vegetation either on the ground or above it in grass, sedge, shrubs, or trees. Their diet includes seeds, flowers, cactus fruit, succulent green sprouts, and invertebrates. Weight varies among species from 6 to 20 grams (0.2 to 0.7 ounce) and body length from 5 to 15 cm (1.9 to 5.9 inches); the slender, scantily haired tail may be either shorter or longer than the body. Fur is soft and ranges in colour from pale buff gray to shades of brown or blackish, with underparts of white or gray, sometimes tinted with buff.

New World harvest mice belong to the subfamily Sigmodontinae of the mouse family Muridae within the order Rodentia. Their ancestry is seen in the North American geologic record back to the early Pliocene Epoch (5.3 million to 3.6 million years ago). Their closest living relatives are deer mice.

Old World Harvest Mouse

The single species of Old World harvest mouse (*Micromys minutus*) lives from Great Britain and Europe westward to Siberia and Korea, southern China, Assam, and Japan. As suggested by its scientific name, it is among the smallest of rodents, weighing less than 7 grams (0.25 ounce) and having a body length of less than 8 cm (3.1 inches). The semi-prehensile tail is about the same length as the body and is scantily haired. The soft fur is brownish yellow to reddish brown above, white to buff on the underparts.

Old World harvest mouse (Micromys minutus). John Markham

The Old World harvest mouse is an agile climber that prefers tall vegetation such as hedgerows, grasses, reeds, bamboo, and cultivated grain or rice fields. It is active all year and is primarily but not entirely nocturnal. During breeding season this mouse constructs globular nests of grass suspended between vertical stems up to 13 cm (5.1 inches) above ground; during the rest of the year, nests are located in holes in the ground, beneath haystacks, or in buildings. The Old World harvest mouse eats seeds and other vegetation in addition to insects and the eggs of small birds. Modern farm machinery may be destroying the animal's food and nesting resources in Great Britain and Europe, where populations are apparently declining.

The Old World harvest mouse belongs to the subfamily Murinae of the mouse family Muridae. While some investigators recognize only one species of *Micromys*, others speculate that additional species exist. Fossils of six extinct Eurasian species date back as far as the late Pliocene Epoch (3.6 to 2.6 million years ago). Wood mice are the closest living relatives of the Old World harvest mouse.

MEADOW VOLES

Meadow voles (*Microtus pennsylvanicus*), also called meadow mice, are among the most common and prolific small mammals in North America. Weighing less than 50 grams (1.8 ounces), this stout vole is 15 to 20 cm (5.9 to 7.9 inches) long, including its short tail (3 to 6 cm). The dense, soft fur is chestnut-brown above and gray or grayish buff on the underparts; some individuals are much darker.

Primarily terrestrial and active all year, meadow voles can swim but have never been seen climbing. They are more active during the day in habitats with dense cover

Meadow vole (Microtus pennsylvanicus). Judith Myers

and at night when temperatures are high. In addition to meadows, they are found in swampy pastures, fields covered with dead grass and herbs, coastal saline meadows, and sometimes grassy openings in forests. Preferred habitats include moist fields of grass and sedge (especially bluegrass) that provide thick protective cover. They dwell both above and below the ground but spend a higher proportion of time on the surface, traveling along networks of trails and tunnels through meadow vegetation to forage for food. Their diet comprises grasses (including the seeds), sedges, other herbaceous plants, and tender tree bark. Roots, tubers, and other plant parts are cached in a burrow to eat during the winter. Voles construct nests of dry grass either on the ground or at the ends of underground burrows. In swampy areas the nest is placed high and dry in a grass tussock.

Few mammals are more prolific than the meadow vole, which has a gestation period of 20 to 21 days and produces up to 17 litters per year. Depending upon the region, average litter size ranges from 4 to 8 young, with extremes of 1 to 11. Although highly prolific, population increase is curtailed by extremely high predation (especially by weasels, hawks, and owls), short life span, and sometimes disease. Although solitary in the breeding season, they live communally during the winter nonbreeding season.

The meadow vole has the largest geographic distribution of any species of *Microtus* in North America. Its range extends through almost all of Alaska and Canada southward through the Rocky Mountains to New Mexico and eastward across the northern Great Plains to the Atlantic seaboard from Maine to Georgia. Isolated populations are found in western Florida and northern Chihuahua, Mexico.

Some meadow vole populations, particularly those in the northern parts of its range, are cyclical, reaching high densities every two to five years. During such a cycle in

Ontario, Canada, for example, 166 individuals per acre (415 per hectare) were recorded. Factors responsible for such density fluctuations are unknown but are the subject of much ecological research.

The meadow vole is one of 61 species in the genus *Microtus*. Its closest living relative is the beach vole (*M. breweri*) of Muskeget Island off the coast of Massachusetts, which evolved from mainland populations of the meadow vole only during the last 3,000 years. The genus *Microtus* contains about half of all vole species. Voles, lemmings, and muskrats are all classified in the subfamily Arvicolinae within the mouse family Muridae, order Rodentia.

Voles

Voles are small-bodied mouselike rodents of the Northern Hemisphere. Each of the 124 known species has a blunt rather than a tapered muzzle, a tail shorter than the body, and small eyes and ears. Voles live in a wide variety of habitats at elevations ranging from sea level to high mountains. In North America they range from Alaska southward to the mountains of Mexico and Guatemala. In Eurasia they can be found in the British Isles and across Europe and Asia to southern China, Taiwan, and Japan. The only African voles exist as an isolated population in coastal Libya. Habitats exploited by voles include prairies, steppes, semideserts, alpine and subalpine meadows, tree-less tundra, and several types of forest, including cloud, deciduous, and coniferous.

The woodland vole (*Microtus pinetorum*) of the eastern United States is one of the smallest, weighing less than 35 grams (1 ounce) and having a body length up to 10 cm (4 inches) and a tail shorter than 3 cm (1.2 inches). The European water vole (*Arvicola terrestris*) is the largest of the native Eurasian voles, weighing up to 250 grams (8.8 ounces) and having a body up to 22 cm (8.7 inches) long and a tail up to 13 cm (5.1 inches). Depending upon the species, voles' soft, dense fur is generally solid gray, brown, chestnut, or reddish on the upperparts, or reddish brown on the back and gray on the sides. Underparts are paler, ranging from white to gray to brown.

Voles are active year-round. Some species are nocturnal, some are diurnal, and others are active day and night. Their diet consists of plants and occasionally insects and fungi. Some species in some regions can be agricultural pests. Nearly all voles are terrestrial, traveling through tunnels in grass or beneath snow or via elaborate subsurface burrows. There are, however, some dramatic exceptions. Arboreal red and Sonoma tree voles (*Arborimus longicaudus* and *A. pomo*, respectively) are found only in humid coastal old-growth forests of northern California and Oregon, where they live and nest in the tops of Douglas fir, grand fir, and Sitka spruce trees and eat the outer parts of conifer needles (particularly Douglas fir). In mountain meadows of the western United States and Canada, the semiaquatic American water vole (*M. richardsoni*) dwells close to clear spring-fed or glacial streams and the edges of ponds. They are adept swimmers and divers whose pathways extend along and cross over springs and streams. Their burrow entrances may be at water level or submerged. Their diet consists of roots, rhizomes, and preformed buds of perennials. Mole voles (genus *Ellobius*) have tiny eyes and ears and the velvety fur common to burrowing rodents. Mole voles live in deep, moist soil of the steppes and dry grasslands of Central Asia, digging elaborate burrows up to 50 cm (19.7 inches) below ground and eating the underground parts of plants.

Woodland Voles

The woodland vole (*Microtus pinetorum*) inhabits the eastern United States. It is well adapted to burrowing, as reflected by its slender, cylindrical body, strong feet, and large front claws. The very small eyes and ears are hidden in short, dense molelike fur; prominent whiskers are useful in navigating underground.

The woodland vole is one of the smallest members of its genus, weighing 14 to 37 grams (0.5 to 1.3 ounces). It measures 11 to 14 cm (4.3 to 5.5 inches) long, including the short tail (1 to 3 cm [0.4 to 1.2 inches]). The soft, silky fur is glossy brown or chestnut and is darker in the winter than in the summer. The underparts are dusky or silvery gray. The tail is brown above and lighter below.

The woodland vole is active all year, day or night. It spends most of its time in burrows dug just below a ceiling of thick leaf litter. To construct the burrows, the vole first loosens the soil by using its head, incisor teeth, and forefeet. It then turns around and, again using its head, pushes the

Woodland vole (Microtus pinetorum). Shutterstock.com

resulting debris out of the tunnel and into piles under the leaf litter. Woodland voles also build globular nests of dead grass and leaves under logs or within the burrows. They occasionally emerge from their subsurface network, but only long enough to scamper through shallow pathways into another shelter. Their diet consists of grass (both roots and stems), fruit, seeds, and bark; sometimes fungi and insects are eaten. One to four litters are produced each year with one to five young per litter; the average is two or three. Gestation is only about three weeks.

Woodland voles are found from extreme southern Ontario to northern Florida along the eastern seaboard, and westward to central Wisconsin, eastern Kansas and Oklahoma, and northeastern Texas. They are most common in beech-maple forests of the eastern and central states, where moist, crumbly soils support dense grassy patches or thick carpets of leaves. Along coastal bays they live from the edge of the shore to spruce and birch forest in mountains. They inhabit orchards of the northeastern United States and cultivated fields of southern states. Only at the extreme southeastern segment of their range (northern Florida) are they found in dense pine and scrub oak woodlands. Isolated populations in eastern Texas are remnants of a former southwestern distribution, as revealed by cave samples dating from the Pleistocene Epoch (2,600,000 to 11,700 years ago). These samples show that now-arid habitats in the Southwest were once moist grasslands inhabited by woodland voles.

The woodland vole is one of 61 species in the meadow vole genus (*Microtus*). Its closest living relative is the Jalapan pine vole (*M. quasiater*), which inhabits cool and wet forests of eastern Mexico in the states of San Luis Potosí and Oaxaca.

CHAPTER 4
FAMILIAR RODENTS

Although the term *rodent* is typically associated with rats and mice, the order also contains several other diverse groups of mammals. Some of these groups, such as ground squirrels and porcupines, are widely distributed and easily recognized by many people throughout the world. They are separated into solitary and communal species below.

GENERALLY COMMUNAL FORMS

Members of several widespread rodent taxa live in family, or extended family, groups or in colonies. Perhaps the most well known communal rodents are the beavers and prairie dogs, two colonial groups that construct elaborate living spaces.

BEAVERS

Beavers (genus *Castor*) are amphibious rodents native to North America, Europe, and Asia. The two living species are the largest North American and Eurasian rodents, with bodies up to 80 cm (31 inches) long and generally weighing 16–30 kg (35–66 pounds, with the heaviest recorded at more than 38.5 kg [85 pounds]). They live in streams, rivers, marshes, ponds, and shorelines of large lakes, constructing dams of branches, stones, and mud, forming ponds that often cover many hectares.

Beavers have short legs and a stout body with a small, broad, and blunt head. Massive chisel-shaped incisor teeth have orange outer enamel because iron has replaced

Beaver (Castor canadensis). *Master engineers, beavers create dams, lodges, storehouses, and canals.* Shutterstock.com

calcium, making them stronger than most rodent incisors. Upon submergence, folds of skin (valves) close the nostrils and the stubby rounded ears, and the eyes are protected by a membrane that keeps water out (nictitating membrane). The fur-lined lips close behind the incisors, blocking water from the mouth and lungs and allowing the animal to cut, peel, and carry branches underwater. Small front feet with five clawed digits dexterously manipulate food. The hind feet are quite large, and the five digits are connected by webbing, which makes them useful as paddles for propulsion underwater. Claws of the second hind digits are split and have serrated edges used for grooming the fur. Fur consists of a grayish to brown layer of short, fine, and dense underfur that keeps water from reaching the skin. Over this layer are long, coarse, glossy guard hairs ranging in colour from yellowish brown through reddish brown to black; underparts of the animal are paler. The distinctive tail is scaly, flat, and paddle-shaped, measuring up to 45 cm (17.7 inches) long and 13 cm (5.1 inches) wide. Both sexes possess castor glands that exude a musky secretion (castoreum), which is deposited on mud or rocks to mark territorial boundaries. Anal glands secrete oil through skin pores to hair roots. From there it is distributed with the front feet and grooming claws over the whole body to keep the fur sleek, oily, and water-repellent.

Beavers are colonial and primarily nocturnal. Their characteristically dome-shaped island lodges are built of branches plastered with mud. In marshes, lakes, and small rivers, beavers may instead construct bank lodges, and in large rivers and lakes they excavate bank dens with an underwater entrance beneath tree roots or overhanging ledges. Each lodge is occupied by an extended family group of up to eight individuals: an adult pair, young of the year (kits), and yearlings from the previous litter. Lodges are usually 3 metres (10 feet) high and 6 metres (20 feet) across the base but can be as large as 5 metres (about 16 feet) high and 12 metres (39 feet) wide. One or more tunnel entrances open below the water's surface into a spacious central chamber above water level; the floor is covered with vegetation. An entry tunnel leads to the nest chamber above the waterline. In winter the moist walls freeze, adding insulation and making the lodge impenetrable to predators. During winter beavers store some fat at the base of their tail, but they maintain body temperature primarily by huddling in the insulated lodge and being less active. They leave the lodge only to feed on branches cached beneath the ice. Slow swimmers, beavers can remain submerged for up to 15 minutes, propelling themselves primarily with the webbed hind feet while the front feet are held tight against the body. On land they walk or run with a waddling gait. Their diet consists of the soft cambium layer beneath bark, as well as the buds, leaves, and twigs of certain trees (willows and aspens are preferred). Pond vegetation and bankside plants are also eaten. Herbaceous vegetation is consumed mostly during summer and woody matter during winter. Shrubs, saplings, and trees are felled by beavers, cut into portable lengths, and dragged along mud slides or floated through beaver-made canals to the lodge. Edible branches are cached underwater and anchored in mud near the lodge entrance, where they are to be eaten all winter when the beavers cannot break through the ice to cut fresh branches.

Beavers are monogamous, mating between January and March in the north and November or December in the south. One litter per year of one to nine (usually four) kits is born in the spring after a gestation of 105 days. Beavers communicate by postures, vocalization, scent marking, and tail slapping. When alarmed on land, they retreat to water and warn others by slapping the surface of the water with their tails, producing a loud, startling noise. Eagles, large hawks, and most large mammalian carnivores prey on beavers.

American beavers (*C. canadensis*) occur throughout forested parts of North America to northern Mexico, including the southwestern United States and peninsular Florida. Beavers were at the heart of the fur trade during colonial times and contributed significantly to the westward settlement and development of North America and Canada. As the animal was trapped out in the east, trappers moved progressively westward, with settlers following. Nearly made extinct by 1900 through excessive trapping for their luxuriant coat, they have reclaimed, either by natural movement or human reintroduction, much of their former natural range, and regulated trapping continues, particularly in Canada. American beavers have also been introduced into Finland, where they are flourishing.

Eurasian beavers (*C. fiber*) were once found throughout temperate and boreal forests of the region (including Britain) except for the Mediterranean area and Japan. By the early 20th century this range had contracted, and at the beginning of the 21st century indigenous populations survived only in the Elbe and Rhône river drainages, southern Norway, France, Mongolia, China, and parts of Russia, especially northwestern Siberia and the Altai region. Efforts to reestablish the Eurasian species began in Sweden in the early 1920s. Since that time, Eurasian beavers have been reintroduced throughout Europe, western Siberia, western China, Mongolia, the Kamchatka Peninsula, and near the Amur River in the Russian Far East.

Beavers make up the family Castoridae (suborder Sciuromorpha, order Rodentia). With no close living relatives (the mountain beaver belongs to a separate family), modern beavers are remnants of a rich evolutionary history of 24 extinct genera extending back to the Late Eocene Epoch of Asia and the Early Oligocene of Europe and North America. Most were terrestrial burrowers, such as *Palaeocastor*, which is known by fossils from Late Oligocene–Early Miocene sediments of western Nebraska and eastern Wyoming. They probably lived in upland grasslands in large colonies, excavated extensive burrow systems, and grazed on the surface, their entire lifestyle being much like that of modern prairie dogs. The largest rodent that ever lived in North America was the amphibious giant beaver (*Castoroides*) of the Pleistocene Epoch. Fossils indicate that it had a body length of two metres (about 7 feet) and was about the size of a black bear.

GERBILS

Over 110 species of gerbils (subfamily Gerbillinae) are known. Gerbils are African, Indian, and Asian rodents (which also include sand rats and jirds) that inhabit arid habitats. One Mongolian species (*Meriones unguiculatus*) is a gentle and hardy animal that has become a popular pet.

All gerbils have long hind feet and fairly large ears and eyes, but there is variation among other characteristics. Body form varies from stout and compact to slender. One of the largest is the great gerbil (*Rhombomys opimus*), which inhabits the deserts of Central Asia and is 15 to 20 cm (5.9 to 7.9 inches) long, with a slightly shorter, densely haired tail. The smallest is probably *Desmodilliscus braueri* of northern Africa, weighing a mere 6 to 14 grams (0.2 to 0.5 ounce) and measuring 4 to 8 cm (1.6 to 3.1 inches) long, not including the shorter, scantily haired tail.

Most gerbils are nocturnal; a few species, however, are active only in early morning and evening or during the day. Gerbils walk and scamper on all four limbs and flee in running leaps when alarmed. Some construct short, simple burrows, but others construct elaborate underground galleries. The burrows of the great gerbil sometimes weaken embankments in western Asia, where it also damages crops. Although these rodents primarily eat seeds, roots, nuts, green plant parts, and insects, the Indian gerbil (*Tatera indica*) also eats eggs and young birds. Gerbils are active throughout the year, but in regions where winters are cold and snow is usual, they may remain in burrows, feeding on cached food for days or weeks at a time.

Gerbils inhabit open, sparsely vegetated, and often harsh environments such as sandy and rocky deserts and plains, dry steppes, thorny scrub and woodland savannas, and rocky mountain slopes. Their range includes Africa and extends from southern Turkey through the Middle East and the Arabian Peninsula eastward to Mongolia and northern China, peninsular India, and Sri Lanka.

Nearly all gerbils have six upper and six lower cheek teeth, but the fat-tailed gerbil (*Pachyuromys duprasi*) of the Sahara Desert, which eats only insects, has six upper but only four lower cheek teeth, a unique combination among the "true" rats and mice (family Muridae). Its very short and club-shaped tail may be an adaptation for fat storage. The bushy-tailed jird (*Sekeetamys calurus*) of northeastern Africa and adjacent Asia has an extremely bushy tail tipped with white. Depending on the species, gerbils' tails may be much longer than the head and body, about the same length, or shorter. Their fur is soft and dense, sometimes silky, with gray, tan, brown, or reddish brown upperparts and white to grayish underparts. Some species are distinguished by dark markings on the head, others by white or buff patches behind the ears; soles of the hind feet may be hairless or moderately to densely furred.

Gerbils constitute the subfamily Gerbillinae of the family Muridae within the order Rodentia. Their closest relatives are species of the extinct genus *Myocricetodon*, represented by fossils extending back to the Middle Miocene Epoch (16.4 million to 11.2 million years ago) in Africa and Eurasia.

GROUND SQUIRRELS

Ground squirrels encompass any of 62 species of long-bodied terrestrial rodents that are active during the day and have short legs, strong claws, small rounded ears, and a short or moderately long tail. Colour varies widely among species from gray, tawny, or pale brown to olive, reddish, or very dark brown. A few species are solid-coloured, but most exhibit characteristic patterns such as dappling,

California ground squirrel (Spermophilus beecheyi). Kenneth W. Fink/ Root Resources

lines of spots, white to brownish black stripes, bright reddish brown cheeks, or stripes combined with a yellowish red mantle over the head and shoulders. Underparts are white, shades of gray, tones of buff, or brown. In some species individuals may be partially or completely black (melanistic). Fur ranges in texture from harsh and thin to soft and dense and sometimes woolly.

NONTROPICAL GROUND SQUIRRELS

The name *ground squirrel* is typically applied to small rodents that excavate burrows and are associated with open habitats at temperate latitudes in North American and Eurasia as well as arid regions of Africa. The 38 species of North American ground squirrels and Eurasian sousliks (genus *Spermophilus*) are found from sea level to mountaintops in open habitats and occasionally in forests.

The Barbary ground squirrel (*Atlantoxerus getulus*) lives in rocky habitats from sea level to 4,000 metres (13,000 feet) in the Atlas Mountains of northwestern Africa, and the four species of African ground squirrels (genus *Xerus*) inhabit savannas and rocky deserts in northern, eastern, and southern Africa. Central Asia's sandy deserts are home to the single species of long-clawed ground squirrel (genus *Spermophilopsis*), whereas the deserts of the southwestern United States and northern Mexico are populated by five species of antelope ground squirrel (genus *Ammospermophilus*). The white-tailed antelope squirrel (*A. leucurus*) of the southwestern United States is one of the smallest of all ground squirrels, weighing 96 to 117 grams (3.4 to 4 ounces) and having a body up to 17 cm (6.7 inches) long and a tail of less than 8 cm (3.1 inches). One of the largest is the rock squirrel (*Spermophilus variegatus*) of the southwestern United States and northern Mexico. Weighing 450 to 875 grams (30.8 ounces), it has a body up to 30 cm (11.8 inches) long and a somewhat shorter, bushy tail. Members of both these genera have internal cheek pouches, which are used to collect food for storage in burrows.

Most nontropical ground squirrels are omnivorous. Franklin's ground squirrel (*Spermophilus franklinii*) of the north-central United States and southern Canada eats a representative omnivore diet: a wide variety of green plant parts, fruit, insects (caterpillars, grasshoppers, crickets, beetles and their larvae, and ants), vertebrates (toads, frogs, the eggs and chicks of ducks and songbirds, mice, smaller ground squirrels, and small rabbits), and carrion. Others, such as the Uinta ground squirrel (*S. armatus*) of the Rocky Mountains in the western United States, are primarily vegetarian, eating mostly green plant parts and seeds.

Spermophilus species hibernate deeply during winter months. The body temperature of the 13-lined ground squirrel (*S. tridecemlineatus*) of central North America drops from 37 °C (98.6 °F) to 1 to 3 degrees above burrow temperature. During this time the heart rate decreases from 200 to 350 beats per minute in the active animal to about 5, and the respiration rate falls from 50 breaths per minute to about 4.

In contrast, the antelope and African ground squirrels are active all year. These two groups regulate their body temperature by entering and re-emerging from cool burrows during hot parts of the day. Outside the burrow they sit or stand facing away from the sun, their long, wide, and bushy tail serving as a heat shield over the animal's back. Central Asia's long-clawed ground squirrel is also active year-round, remaining in its burrow only on extremely cold winter days.

TROPICAL GROUND SQUIRRELS

Tropical ground squirrels are active all year and do not store food. The five genera (*Dremomys, Lariscus, Menetes, Rhinosciurus*, and *Hyosciurus*) live in the forests of Southeast Asia but not in the Philippines. Although they sometimes utilize holes in the ground, these rodents usually nest in hollow tree trunks and rotting branches on the forest floor. Diet varies among species but generally includes a greater percentage of arthropods than that of nontropical ground squirrels. The shrew-faced ground squirrel (*R. laticaudatus*) of the Sunda Islands, for example, is highly specialized to eat earthworms and insects with its greatly elongated snout, long tongue, and weak incisor teeth. The three-striped ground squirrel (*L. insignis*), also of the Sunda Islands, is reported to eat fruit, roots, and insects; plain long-nosed ground squirrels (genus *Dremomys*) eat fruit, insects, and earthworms. The two species of Sulawesi ground squirrel (genus *Hyosciurus*) have elongated snouts and use their long, strong claws to dig for beetle larvae in rotting wood; they also eat acorns.

CLASSIFICATION

Ground squirrels belong to the subfamily Sciurinae, which includes tree squirrels and chipmunks. Subfamily Sciurinae is part of the squirrel family (Sciuridae) in the order Rodentia. *Atlantoxerus*, *Xerus*, and *Spermophilopsis* are closely related within this subfamily, as are *Ammospermophilus* and *Spermophilus*, which are classified in a subgroup within Sciurinae that includes marmots and prairie dogs. The tropical ground squirrels are most closely related to tropical Asian tree squirrels.

GUINEA PIGS

The guinea pig (*Cavia porcellus*) is a domesticated South American rodent belonging to the cavy family (Caviidae). It resembles other cavies in having a robust body with short limbs, large head and eyes, and short ears. The feet have hairless soles and short, sharp claws; there are four toes on the forefeet, three on the hind feet. Domestic guinea pigs are fairly large, weighing 500 to 1,500 grams (roughly 1 to 3 pounds) and having a body 20 to 40 cm (8 to 16 inches) long; the tail is not visible externally. There is a crest of longer hairs at the neck, but length and texture of the fur vary from smooth (short or long) to coarse and short or long and silky. Coloration is extremely variable: the coat may

Guinea pigs (Cavia porcellus). Joe B. Blossom/EB Inc.

be white, cream, tan, reddish or chocolate brown, black, or a combined pattern.

Guinea pigs eat vegetation and do not require water to drink if supplied with sufficiently moist food, but they must have water if fed dry commercial food. They breed all year in captivity, with females bearing up to 13 young per litter (4 is average); gestation takes 68 days. Although the young can scamper about and eat solid food the day they are born, they are not fully weaned for about three weeks. Females mature in two months, males in three, and captive guinea pigs live up to eight years, although three to five is typical.

No natural population of this species exists in the wild. Guinea pigs were apparently domesticated more than 3,000 years ago in Peru, coinciding with humans' transition from a nomadic to an agricultural lifestyle. The Incas kept guinea pigs, and the animals were bred during the same period by tribes along the Andes Mountains from northwestern Venezuela to central Chile. These rodents remain a sustainable food source for the native peoples of Ecuador, Peru, and Bolivia, who either keep them in their homes or allow them to scavenge freely both indoors and out. Guinea pigs were taken to Europe in the 16th century, and since the 1800s they have been popular as pets. They are also used internationally as laboratory animals for studies of anatomy, nutrition, genetics, toxicology, pathology, serum development, and other research programs.

There are four other, nondomesticated members of the genus *Cavia* that are also called guinea pigs: the Brazilian guinea pig (*C. aperea*) found from Colombia, Venezuela, and the Guianas south to northern Argentina; the shiny guinea pig (*C. fulgida*) inhabiting eastern Brazil; the montane guinea pig (*C. tschudii*) ranging from Peru to northern Chile and northwestern Argentina; and the greater guinea pig (*C. magna*) occurring in southeastern

Brazil and Uruguay. Breeding and molecular studies suggest that the domestic guinea pig was derived from one of the wild Brazilian, shiny, or montane species.

MARMOTS

Marmots (genus *Marmota*) are giant ground squirrels found primarily in North America and Eurasia. Each of the 14 known species is large and heavy, weighing 3 to 7 kg (6.6 to 15.4 pounds), depending upon the species. Marmots are well suited for life in cold environments and have small fur-covered ears, short, stocky legs, and strong claws for digging. Length of the bulky body is 30 to 60 cm (11.8 to 23.6 inches), and the short, bushy tail is 10 to 25 cm (3.9 to 9.8 inches) long. Their long, thick fur is slightly coarse and may be yellowish brown (usually frosted with

Olympic marmot (Marmota olympus). E.R. Degginger

buff white), brown, reddish brown, black, or a mixture of gray and white.

Marmots are found north of Mexico and in Eurasia from the European Alps through north-central Asia, the Himalayas, and northeastern Siberia to the Kamchatka Peninsula. They inhabit open country in mountains and plains, preferring montane meadows, steppes, tundra, and forest edges. All live in burrows that they excavate, and most mountain species construct burrows beneath boulder fields, rocky slopes, and crevices in cliff faces. This terrain provides protection from predators such as grizzly bears, which are aggressive diggers and a significant predator of the Alaska marmot (*Marmota broweri*) in the Brooks Range. Rocks and cliffs also serve as observation sites where the rodents sit upright watching for both terrestrial and aerial predators. When alarmed, marmots

Hoary marmot (Marmota caligata) *looking over a rock ledge on Mount Rainier, Washington, U.S.* © Jeremy D. Rogers

emit a sharp, piercing whistle and scurry to their burrows if danger persists.

Marmots are active during the day and are almost entirely vegetarian. The Alaska marmot, which grazes on low-nutrient tundra vegetation, must seek productive foraging areas where it competes indirectly with other mammalian grazers, including caribou, Dall's sheep, and voles. Some marmots, such as the Alpine marmot (*M. marmota*) and the hoary marmot (*M. caligata*) of northwestern North America, are gregarious and social, but others, including the woodchuck (*M. monax*) of Canada and the United States, are solitary. All hibernate in winter, most of them deeply, although some may emerge from their burrows for short periods on mild winter days. During hibernation they live on fat reserves accumulated during the summer. The hoary marmot hibernates for up to nine months, its fat reserves amounting to 20 percent of its total body weight. Marmots mate soon after they emerge from hibernation. Gestation lasts about a month, and a litter of generally 4 or 5 (recorded extremes range from 2 to 11) is born in a nest within the burrow. Most marmots produce young every year, but the Olympic marmot (*M. olympus*) of the Olympic Mountains in the United States bears young every other year.

Marmots belong to the squirrel family (Sciuridae) within the order Rodentia. The closest living relatives of marmots are ground squirrels and prairie dogs. Marmots' evolutionary history is recorded in North America by fossils of extinct species from the late Miocene Epoch (13.8 million to 5.3 million years ago). In Eurasia there is no evidence earlier than the Pleistocene Epoch (2.6 million to 11,700 years ago).

MUSKRATS

Muskrats (*Ondatra zibethicus*) are large amphibious rodents indigenous to North America but found also in

Europe, Ukraine, Russia, Siberia, adjacent areas of China and Mongolia, and Honshu Island in Japan. The muskrat is a robust vole weighing up to 1.8 kg (4 pounds). It has short legs and a compact body up to 33 cm (13 inches) long. The scaly, sparsely haired tail is flattened vertically and can be as long as the body. The eyes are small, and the ears are nearly concealed by fur, which ranges in colour from reddish to blackish brown and consists of a short, soft underfur heavily overlaid with long, stiff, glossy guard hairs. The dense underfur traps air, providing both insulation and buoyancy. Muskrats' large hind feet, fringed with stiff bristles and partially webbed, are used as oars when swimming, with the tail serving as a rudder. They can stay submerged for up to 20 minutes and swim as fast as 5 km (3.1 miles) per hour. The animal is named for the musky odour of a yellowish substance produced by perineal glands. Secreted into the urine, the substance is used to mark lodges, pathways, and other landmarks throughout an individual's home range.

Marshes are the usual habitat of muskrats, but they also live in wooded swamps, lakes, and streams, where they build sizable lodges of cattails, sedges, and other vegetation. They also dig burrows near the water's edge for shelter, and their burrowing sometimes weakens earthen dams and dikes. Eating mostly grasses and cattails, muskrats consume the roots and stalks of a wide variety of other aquatic plants; they are, however, occasionally predatory, taking freshwater mussels, snails, crustaceans, salamanders, fish, and young birds for food. Females produce one or more litters of three to eight young each year after a gestation period of three to four weeks.

The muskrat's indigenous geographic range covers most of North America south of the tundra from Alaska to Newfoundland into the southern United States. It does not occur in Florida or coastal parts of Georgia and South

Carolina; British Columbia and California have nonnative populations, although Baja California has an indigenous population. In South America the muskrat was introduced into southern Argentina. It is widespread in Eurasia owing to the introduction of several populations during the early 1900s. Historically, the muskrat was trapped for its thick and durable coat, and it is still sought by the fur trade. Muskrat flesh has been sold as "marsh rabbit."

The Florida water rat (*Neofiber alleni*) is sometimes called the round-tailed muskrat. It resembles a small muskrat (up to 38 cm [15 inches] in total length), but its tail is round rather than flat. This animal is less aquatic than *Ondatra* and lives in the grassy marshes and prairies of Florida and southeastern Georgia. Both belong to the subfamily Arvicolinae of the mouse family (Muridae) within the order Rodentia.

PRAIRIE DOGS

Prairie dogs (genus *Cynomys*) are burrowing, colony-forming squirrels that inhabit plains, high plateaus, and montane valleys in North America. Their short, coarse fur is grizzled yellowish buff to reddish or rich cinnamon. Each of the five species of prairie dogs has a short tail, small rounded ears, and short legs with long, strong claws. These rodents weigh up to 1.7 kg (3.7 pounds), with a body 28–33 cm (11–13 inches) long. The slightly flattened tail is 3–12 cm (1.2–4.7 inches) long, and, depending on the species, its tip is black, white, or fringed with white around a gray centre.

Prairie dogs excavate elaborate burrow systems with many entrances marked by low or volcano-shaped mounds. The common black-tailed (*C. ludovicianus*) and Mexican (*C. mexicanus*) species live in large, dense colonies that early explorers described as "towns." Colonies are divided by topographic and vegetational features into semidiscrete wards formed from smaller extended family groups, or coteries. Colonies usually cover about 100 hectares (247 acres), but the largest ever recorded was a black-tailed prairie dog colony in Texas that formerly stretched across 65,000 square km (25,000 square miles) and contained an estimated 400 million individuals.

During the day, foraging above ground is the principal activity. Succulent parts of herbs and grasses, leaves, and new shrub growth are eaten in the spring, and seeds are the primary component of the summer diet, with stems and roots being the mainstay in fall and early winter. The black-tailed and Mexican prairie dogs do not hibernate and are periodically active during winter; they do not store food in their burrows. During winter when food is scarce, black-tails remain in their burrows for long periods without food or water, using physiological adaptations to control their metabolism. The other three species become torpid in October or November and emerge in March or April. Late winter or early spring is the breeding season for all species, and after about a month's gestation, females drop a litter of up to 10 young. Communication takes the form of alarm calls (repetitious barks and chuckles), threats (snarls, growls, and tooth chatters), and distress calls (screaming);

Black-tailed prairie dog (Cynomys ludovicianus). Leonard Lee Rue III

individuals enhance group cohesion by greeting one another upon contact, using vocalizations that are specific to each species.

Natural predators of prairie dogs include badgers, wolves, coyotes, bobcats, black-footed ferrets, golden eagles, and large hawks. Once abundant, prairie dog populations have been drastically reduced in range and number by poisoning programs of ranchers who have considered them as pests and by conversion of habitat to cropland. The black-tailed prairie dog (*C. ludovicianus*) is the most widespread, living throughout the Great Plains from Canada to northern Mexico; Gunnison's prairie dog (*Cynomys gunnisoni*) occurs where Arizona, Colorado, New Mexico, and Utah meet; the white-tailed prairie dog (*C. leucurus*) is found from eastern Wyoming through intermontane Rocky Mountain valleys to the eastern margin of the Great Basin; the Utah prairie dog (*C. parvidens*) is restricted to the southern part of that state; and the Mexican prairie dog (*C. mexicanus*) occurs in northern Mexico.

The genus *Cynomys* belongs to the squirrel family (Sciuridae) of rodents (order Rodentia) and is most closely related to North American and Eurasian ground squirrels (genus *Spermophilus*). Fossils document their evolutionary history in western North America since the late Pliocene Epoch (3.6 million to 2.6 million years ago).

SQUIRRELS

All squirrels belong to the family Sciuridae. The 268 squirrel species are classified across 50 genera. The common name is derived from the Greek *skiouros*, meaning "shade tail," which describes one of the most conspicuous and recognizable features of these small mammals. These distinctive animals occupy a range of ecological niches worldwide

New York City, where the squirrel is the official mascot of the NYC Parks Department, is home to many thousands of squirrels. This one was photographed in Manhattan's Gramercy Park. Hope Lourie Killcoyne

virtually anywhere there is vegetation. The squirrel family includes ground squirrels, chipmunks, marmots, prairie dogs, and flying squirrels, but to most people *squirrel* refers to the 122 species of tree squirrels, which belong to 22 genera of the subfamily Sciurinae. The North American gray squirrel (*Sciurus carolinensis*) has adapted to urban and suburban areas where it is regarded as aesthetic or as a minor annoyance. In northern Europe the red squirrel (*S. vulgaris*) is valued for its soft, thick fur. Villagers in tropical forests keep squirrels as pets. Most species are hunted for food. The North American red squirrel (*Tamiasciurus hudsonicus*), also known as a pine squirrel or a chickaree, is somewhat larger than a chipmunk, and primarily feeds on the seeds of conifers (evergreen trees and shrubs).

General Features

Tree squirrels have slender, lanky bodies, long, muscular limbs, and furred feet. The forefeet have four long digits plus a short, stubby thumb, and the five-toed hind feet are narrow or moderately wide. The bald soles of the feet take the form of prominent, fleshy pads. Because the ankle joints are flexible and can be rotated, squirrels can rapidly descend trees headfirst with the hind feet splayed flat against the trunk. Their large, bright eyes convey an alert demeanour, and the broad, short head tapers to a blunt muzzle adorned with long whiskers. The rounded ears, small in relation to body size, are densely covered with short, fine hairs, which form a long tuft at the tips of the ears in some species. The tail is about as long as head and body or appreciably longer. Furred from base to tip, the tail appears bushy and cylindrical when the hairs grow evenly around the tail; the tail appears flatter if the fur originates only from opposite sides. Claws are large, strong, curved, and very sharp, which enables tree squirrels to navigate vertical surfaces and slim branches.

Variation in body size is considerable. Largest are the four species of Oriental giant squirrels (genus *Ratufa*) native to the tropical forests of Southeast Asia. Weighing 1.5 to 3 kg (3 to almost 7 pounds), it has a body length of 25 to 46 cm (about 10 to 18 inches) and a tail about as long. Two species of pygmy squirrels are the smallest: the neotropical pygmy squirrel (*Sciurillus pusillus*) of the Amazon Basin weighs 33 to 45 grams (1 to 1.5 ounces), with a body 9 to 12 cm (3.5 to 4.7 inches) long and an equally long tail; but the African pygmy squirrel (*Myosciurus pumilio*) of the West African tropical forests is even smaller, at 13 to 20 grams (0.5 to 0.7 ounce), with a body length of 6 to 8 cm (2.4 to 3.1 inches) and a somewhat shorter tail.

Squirrels' soft, dense fur is moderately long in most species but can be very long and almost shaggy in some.

Colour is extraordinarily variable. Some species are plain, covered in one or two solid shades of brown or gray. A few species are striped along the sides and back; sometimes the head is also striped. Tropical species exhibit combinations of white, gray, yellow, orange, red, maroon, brown, and black, yielding a variety of complex coat patterns.

NATURAL HISTORY

All tree squirrels are diurnal and arboreal, but the range of vertical activity in species differs widely, especially among those living in tropical rainforests. Some, such as the Oriental giant squirrels (genus *Ratufa*) and the African giant squirrels (genus *Protoxerus*), rarely descend from the high canopy. Others, such as the pygmy squirrel of Sulawesi (*Prosciurillus murinus*), travel and forage at intermediate levels between ground and canopy. Some large tropical squirrels, such as the Sulawesi giant squirrel (*Rubrisciurus rubriventer*) and the northern Amazon red squirrel (*Sciurus igniventris*), nest at middle levels but travel and forage low in the understory or on the ground. The African palm squirrels (genus *Epixerus*) are long-legged runners that forage only on the ground. Certain species, such as the red-tailed squirrel (*S. granatensis*) of the American tropics and the African pygmy squirrel, are active from ground to canopy. In the United States, the Eastern fox squirrel (*S. niger*) runs along the ground from tree to tree, but others, including the Eastern gray squirrel (*S. carolinensis*), prefer to travel through the treetops and regularly cross rivers by swimming with the head up and tail flat on the water's surface. Thomas's rope squirrel (*Funisciurus anerythrus*) of Africa even submerges itself and swims underwater.

Most tree squirrels have strong chisel-like incisors and powerful jaws, which are required for gnawing open the hard nuts that, along with fruits, are a primary component of their diet. They also eat seeds, fungi, insects and other arthropods, the cambium layer of tree bark, nectar, leaves, buds, flowers, and sometimes bird eggs, nestlings, and carrion. Some red squirrels (genus *Tamiasciurus*) and *Sciurus* species of temperate climates will stalk, kill, and eat other squirrels, mice, and adult birds and rabbits for food, but such predation in tropical tree squirrels seems rare.

Nests are constructed among branches in the forest canopy or at lower levels in tree crowns, vine tangles, tree hollows, or undergrowth near the ground. Some species of tropical tree squirrels produce several litters per year; breeding season in the Northern Hemisphere may extend from December to September and may result in one or two litters that average three to seven young, depending upon the species.

In the New World, tree squirrels range from the boreal forests of Canada and Alaska southward through coniferous and deciduous woodlands in the United States to the tropical rainforests of South America. In Africa, tree squirrels are native to rainforests and some woodland savannas. Their distribution in the remainder of the Old World extends from the northern boreal forests of Europe and Asia to the Indonesian tropical rainforests. East of the Asian continental margin, tree squirrels inhabit the forests of Taiwan, some islands in the Philippines, and Sulawesi, but they do not occur naturally anywhere east of those islands. Most of the species in 20 of the 22 genera are found in tropical rainforests.

Evolutionary History

Tree squirrels belong to the subfamily Sciurinae; it and the subfamily Pteromyinae (flying squirrels) constitute the family Sciuridae of the order Rodentia. Fossils record the evolutionary history of tree squirrels back to the Late Eocene Epoch (41.3 million to 33.7 million years ago) in North America and the Miocene Epoch (23.8 million to 5.3 million years ago) in Africa and Eurasia.

GROUPS WITH GENERALLY SOLITARY MEMBERS

Several familiar rodents lead generally solitary lifestyles. Members of some groups, such as the mountain beavers and pocket gophers, interact with others of their kind only during breeding season, preferring to hunt, forage, and live alone for the remainder of the year. Hamsters are among the most notable hermits.

CHIPMUNKS

Chipmunks (genus *Tamias*) are rodents that belong to the squirrel family Sciuridae. Each of the 25 known species has a striped, terrestrial form that possesses large internal

The reddish brown eastern chipmunk lives in the forests of eastern North America. Ken Brate/Photo Researchers

cheek pouches used for transporting food. They have prominent eyes and ears, a furry tail, and delicate claws. All are active only during the day, and all but one are North American, occurring from southern Canada to west-central Mexico. Body length among most species ranges from 8 to 16 cm (3.1 to 6.3 inches) and tail length from 6 to 14 cm (2.4 to 5.5 inches).

Chipmunks are basically pygmy squirrels adapted to exploiting the resources of rocky terrain and forest understories. They scamper along the ground but are also expert climbers. As a group they are an ecologically versatile genus. Different species can be found from sea level to 3,900 metres (12,800 feet) in environments defined by large rocks, boulders, and cliffs. They inhabit various forest types, from timberline slopes and rock-bordered alpine meadows downward through coniferous and deciduous forests to dry scrublands and sagebrush deserts.

The eastern chipmunk (*Tamias striatus*), common to the deciduous forests of eastern North America, is the largest. Weighing 70–142 grams (2.5–5 ounces), it has a body 14–19 cm (5.5–7.5 inches) long and a shorter tail (8–11 cm [3.2 to 4.3 inches]). The fur is reddish brown and is broken by five dark brown stripes running lengthwise down the body. These alternate with two gray-brown stripes and two whitish stripes. The smallest chipmunk is the least chipmunk (*T. minimus*), which weighs about half as much as the eastern chipmunk. The Hopi chipmunk (*T. rufus*) lives among the buttes and canyonlands of the American Southwest and is remarkably adept at climbing sheer rock faces and overhangs. The Uinta chipmunk (*T. umbrinus*), which lives in montane forests of the western United States, is much like a tree squirrel in its habits. In addition to denning in burrows, it regularly sleeps and nests in trees, where it sometimes raises young in tree cavities or abandoned bird nests. The only Old World species is the Siberian chipmunk (*T. sibiricus*), which ranges from the White Sea of northwestern Russia eastward through Siberia to northern Japan and south to China.

The chipmunks' call is a shrill chirring or chipping. They relish seeds, berries, and tender plants, but they also eat fungi, insects and other arthropods, and sometimes carrion. They stuff seeds and nuts into their cheek pouches and carry them to a burrow to be stored for later use. As most chipmunks do not accumulate significant fat during the fall, they depend upon this cached food during the winter. Although they experience periods of torpor, chipmunks occasionally emerge on sunny, windless winter days. They were not considered to be true hibernators, but studies now indicate that the eastern chipmunk's body temperature ranges from 35 to 41 °C (95 to 105.8 °F) during activity but drops to 5–7 °C (41–44.6 °F) during torpor—a difference that characterizes true hibernators. Two to eight (rarely nine) young are born in spring or summer after about a month's gestation. A second litter, usually smaller, is often produced in regions with long summers.

HAMSTERS

Eighteen species of Eurasian rodents are classified as hamsters (subfamily Cricetinae). All possess internal cheek pouches. The golden hamster (*Mesocricetus auratus*) of Syria is commonly kept as a pet. Hamsters are stout-bodied, with tails much shorter than body length and have small, furry ears, short, stocky legs, and wide feet. Their thick, long fur ranges from grayish to reddish brown, depending upon the species; underparts are white to shades of gray and black. The Dzhungarian hamster (*Phodopus sungorus*) and the striped dwarf hamster (*Cricetulus barabensis*) have a dark stripe down the middle of the back. Dwarf desert hamsters (genus *Phodopus*) are smallest, with bodies 5 to 10 cm (about

2 to 4 inches) long; the largest is the common hamster (*Cricetus cricetus*), measuring up to 34 cm (13.4 inches) long, not including a short tail of up to 6 cm (2.4 inches).

Hamsters are generally solitary and primarily nocturnal, although they are sometimes active in the early morning or late evening. They do not climb but are excellent diggers, constructing burrows with one or more entrances and with galleries that are connected to chambers for nesting, food storage, and other activities. They also appropriate tunnels made by other mammals; the striped hairy-footed hamster (*P. sungorus*), for instance, uses paths and burrows of the pika. Their diet consists mostly of grains but also includes fruit, roots, green parts of plants, invertebrates, and other small animals. Hamsters carry food in their spacious cheek pouches to cache in the burrow. None hibernates during winter, but some experience periods of torpor lasting from a few days to several weeks. Breeding season is from April to October, with two to five litters of 1 to 13 young being born after a gestation period of 13 to 22 days.

Hamsters' northern range extends from central Europe through Siberia, Mongolia, and northern China to Korea. The southern portion of their range stretches from Syria to Pakistan. Throughout dry, open country they inhabit desert borders, vegetated sand dunes, shrubby and rocky foothills and plateaus, river valleys, and mountain steppes; some live among cultivated crops. Geographic distribution varies greatly between species. The common hamster, for example, is found from central Europe to western Siberia and northwestern China, but the golden hamster has been found only near a small town in northwestern Syria.

The 7 genera and 18 species of hamsters form the subfamily Cricetinae of the "true" mouse and rat family Muridae within the order Rodentia. Their evolutionary history is recorded by 15 extinct fossil genera and extends back 11.2 million to 16.4 million years to the Middle Miocene Epoch in Europe and North Africa; in Asia it extends 6 million to 11 million years. Four of the seven living genera include extinct species. One extinct hamster of *Cricetus*, for example, lived in North Africa during the Middle Miocene, but the only extant member of that genus is the common hamster of Eurasia.

GOLDEN HAMSTERS

Many pet enthusiasts might recognize the golden hamster (*Mesocricetus auratus*). Like other hamsters, it has a stout body with short, stocky legs and short, wide feet with small, sharp claws. The head has small, furry ears and huge internal cheek pouches that open inside the lips

Golden or Syrian hamster (Mesocricetus auratus). Shutterstock.com

and extend to behind the shoulders. The tail is stubby and can be either white or pink.

Golden hamsters are small rodents, usually weighing more than 100 grams (about 3.5 ounces) and having a body length up to 18 cm (7.1 inches); females are usually larger than males. In wild populations and in animals designated "normal variety" by breeders, the short fur is dense and very soft, with golden brown upperparts and white or cream underparts extending up onto the body behind the head. More than 120 varieties have been bred for particular coat types. The result is a bewildering range of fur colours, patterns, and texture combinations.

The natural range of the golden hamster is restricted to a region in northwestern Syria around the town of Halab ("Mount Aleppo region" is regularly used in the pet literature). Here the animal inhabits dry, rocky, and shrubby plains or slopes. In 1930 a small group of golden hamsters was transported from Syria to Palestine, and descendants were distributed worldwide. Another group was captured in Syria in 1971 and taken to the United States. Although golden hamsters have not been domesticated, they are docile and have become a popular pet as well as the subject of zoo exhibits and biological research.

In their natural habitat, golden hamsters are solitary and primarily nocturnal, denning in burrows that they construct themselves. Their diet consists of seeds, fruit, and other plant parts, carrion, and invertebrates. Food is transported in the cheek pouches and is stored in burrows for use when they awake from bouts of torpor during cold months. Hamsters do not experience deep hibernation unless it is experimentally induced under laboratory conditions. In captivity these hamsters are bred at about four months old. Gestation lasts 16 to 19 days, and females produce up to five litters per year, each containing up to 16 young, although 6 to 8 is usual. The blind, hairless young weigh 2 to 3 grams (0.1 ounce) at birth and are weaned at about three weeks. If the mother senses danger during the first few days after birth, she may shelter the babies in her cheek pouches. Captive golden hamsters usually live for two years, sometimes three.

The golden hamster is one of four living species in the genus *Mesocricetus*, but there are several other genera that belong to the hamster subfamily (Cricetinae), which is classified in the mouse family (Muridae) of the order Rodentia. Other members of the genus *Mesocricetus* are Brandt's hamster (*M. brandti*), found in southern Turkey, Lebanon, and Israel eastward through Syria to northwestern Iran; the Romanian hamster (*M. newtoni*) is exclusive to eastern Romania and Bulgaria; the Ciscaucasian hamster (*M. raddei*) inhabits the steppes along the northern slopes of the Caucasus Mountains.

MOUNTAIN BEAVERS

Mountain beavers (*Aplodontia rufa*), which are also called sewellels, are muskrat-sized burrowing rodents found only in the Pacific Northwest of North America. Unlike the American and Eurasian beavers (genus *Castor*), the mountain beaver has an extremely short tail and is less than a half metre (1.6 feet) in length; weight is less than 2 kg (4.4 pounds).

It is characterized by small rounded ears, small eyes, short and robust limbs with five digits on each foot, and a white spot under the ears. All digits except the thumb (pollex) end in long, curved, sharp

Mountain beaver (Aplodontia rufa). Drawing by H. Douglas Pratt

claws; the thumb is partially opposable and bears a nail. The animal is dark grayish to reddish brown on the upperparts and gray beneath, its short coat composed of a dense underfur with scattered guard hairs. Mountain beavers are solitary and have acute tactile and olfactory senses but limited ability to see and hear. Their vocalizations are limited to a soft whining, sobbing sound when in pain, grating produced by the teeth, and a high squeal when fighting.

The range of the mountain beaver consists of four disjunct regions: one extending from southern British Columbia to the northern tip of California, another at Mount Shasta and along the western slopes of the Sierra Nevada mountains, and two tiny populations north of San Francisco Bay along the California coast. Here they live in wet forests and meadows at all elevations below the treeline wherever the soil is deep. They are good swimmers and especially prefer areas near seeps and streams in the understories of brambly thickets. Although active night and day, mountain beavers are rarely found far from the entrances of their extensive burrow systems. They construct tunnels 13–18 cm (5–7 inches) high and 15–25 cm wide that radiate from nest sites, food-storage chambers, and numerous openings to the surface. Most burrowing occurs during the summer months, and aboveground activity nearly ceases in winter. However, the mountain beaver does not hibernate and travels through burrows made in the snow. Mating occurs during this time, with a usual litter of two or three kits appearing from February to April after about one month's gestation. During summer, mountain beavers eat most species of ferns along with leaves of shrubs and deciduous trees, then shift to bark and seedlings of conifers and deciduous trees. Also eaten are bracken fern, devil's club, stinging nettle, and rhododendron, which are toxic or unpalatable to other animals. Occasionally mountain beavers climb trees, where they will chew off twigs up to six metres (20 feet) from the ground. In August, mountain beavers pile vegetation near burrow entrances until it becomes wilted or dry, then move it into the burrow to be eaten or used as nest lining.

Aplodontia rufa is the sole remaining species of the family Aplodontidae (suborder Sciuromorpha, order Rodentia). It is relict from a diverse evolutionary history (three families and 34 genera) extending back to the Eocene Epoch (55.8 million to 33.9 million years ago) of North America; some now-extinct forms also lived during Oligocene to Miocene times in Europe and Asia. Fossils of the living species come from Late Pleistocene sediments in northern California, within its modern range. The mountain beaver is more closely related to squirrels (family Sciuridae) than to beavers (family Castoridae) or any other living rodent.

POCKET GOPHERS

Pocket gophers are 38 species of predominantly North and Central American rodents named for their large, fur-lined cheek pouches. They constitute the family Geomyidae within the order Rodentia. The "pockets" open externally on each side of the mouth and extend from the face to the shoulders; they can be everted for cleaning. The lips can be closed behind the protruding, chisel-like upper front teeth, which thereby allows the gopher to excavate soil without ingesting it. Thickset and cylindrical, pocket gophers are 12 to 35 cm (4.7 to 13.8 inches) in body length, with a short neck, small eyes and ears, and short legs. The five front digits on each muscular foreleg bear long and powerful digging claws. The short, sparsely haired tail is sensitive and well supplied with blood vessels and nerves.

Coat colour varies among species from almost white through tones of yellow and brown to black.

Pocket gophers excavate long shallow, winding tunnels to obtain roots and tubers. Burrows for nesting and food storage, however, are deep and extensive and are marked by conspicuous mounds of earth near the entrances. Pocket gophers dig primarily with their front claws and use their front teeth to cut roots and loosen soil or rocks. When moving backward through tunnels, they arch the tail so that its sensitive tip touches the tunnel wall. This allows the pocket gopher to run backward nearly as fast as it can forward.

Occasionally, gophers venture short distances from their burrows to collect succulent herbs, cutting the plants into short pieces and carrying them back in their cheek pouches. Pocket gophers do not hibernate, and stems, roots, and tubers that they hoard in storage chambers enable them to survive the winter. These solitary, pugnacious animals tolerate company only during the breeding season in spring or early summer. About four weeks after mating, the female produces a litter of two to six, and she cares for her blind, hairless young for about six weeks. Then the offspring begin to develop rapidly, and in several more weeks they leave the mother's burrow to excavate their own shelters.

Pocket gophers range from southern Canada and the United States (mostly west of 90° longitude and in Florida), south through Mexico and Central America, to northwestern Colombia. They can be found from coastal areas to above the timberline in high mountains. Between these extremes of elevation, they live in a great variety of habitats from tropical lowlands and grasslands to oak and coniferous forest to mountain meadows.

The closest living relatives of pocket gophers are kangaroo rats and pocket mice. The evolutionary history of Geomyidae is based on fossils of nine extinct genera found only in North American sediments from the Early Oligocene Epoch (33.7 million to 28.5 million years ago).

PORCUPINES

Porcupines are large, herbivorous, quill-bearing rodents that are active from early evening to dawn. All 25 species have short, stocky legs, but their tails range from short to long, with some being prehensile. The quills, or spines, take various forms depending on the species, but all are modified hairs embedded in skin musculature. Old World porcupines (Hystricidae) have quills embedded in clusters, whereas in New World porcupines (Erethizontidae) single quills are interspersed with bristles, underfur, and hair. No porcupine can throw its quills, but they detach easily and will remain embedded in an attacker. Base coloration ranges from grayish brown through dark brown to blackish, but this colouring is overlaid by variegated patterns of white, yellow, orange, or black due to bands on the spines.

New World Porcupines (Family Erethizontidae)

The North American porcupine (*Erethizon dorsatum*) is the largest species in the family, usually weighing less than 7 kg (15.4 pounds) though males occasionally grow significantly larger. Its body is up to 80 cm (31 inches) long, with a tail up to 30 cm (11.8 inches). Both are covered with a total of 30,000 or more hollow quills. On the ground the porcupine ambles along and cannot jump; in the trees it climbs slowly but has excellent balance; in the water it swims well. When approached, the animal presents its rear. If attacked, it will drive its powerful, muscular tail against the assailant. Those who fish, however, are able to prey upon porcupines by attacking their underside; bobcats and wolverines also are known to hunt porcupines successfully.

North American porcupine (Erethizon dorsatum). *Contrary to popular belief, the porcupine cannot shoot its quills, but they do detach easily. Once embedded in the flesh, the quills are quite painful.* Shutterstock.com

The North American porcupine inhabits forests, including wooded areas along rivers in tundra, grassland, and desert regions. Its range extends from Canada to northern Mexico, although it is absent from the southeastern United States. It is sometimes seen during the day, and it is the only New World porcupine that is terrestrial as well as arboreal. It will roost in trees but also dens in hollow trees, logs, or stumps, in addition to caves, rock crevices, burrows, or snowbanks. Individuals living in coniferous forests spend much time on the ground. Those living in deciduous and mixed forests, however, are more often seen in the trees, which are their source of food. During spring and summer, their diet includes buds, twigs, roots, stems, leaves, flowers, berries, seeds, and nuts. In winter, evergreen needles and the cambium layer and inner bark of trees become important sources of food. Bones and antlers are gnawed upon for calcium and other minerals. Although porcupines do not hibernate during the winter, they remain in their dens during especially cold or inclement weather. They are generally solitary but sometimes den in groups.

All other New World porcupines are arboreal, living in tropical forests from southern Mexico to South America. Their muzzles are large and rounded. The stump-tailed porcupine, *Echinoprocta rufescens*, is one of the smallest at 37 cm (14.6 inches) plus a short tail. New World porcupines primarily eat fruit at night and rest during the day in hollow trees or crouch on branches or in tangles of woody vines. Their digits bear long, curved claws, and most species have long, muscular tails that can be curled upward and twisted around branches. Further improving the tail's grip are stiff bristles on the lower surface of its tip (the upper surface is hairless). Still, like their northern relative, these tropical porcupines move slowly and are unable to jump, so they must descend to the ground to cross gaps between trees. The hollow quills of New World porcupines are sharp, stiff, and circular in cross section and have barbed tips. New World porcupines bear usually one young, sometimes two, after about 200 days' gestation.

Old World Porcupines (Family Hystricidae)

Old World species are primarily terrestrial, although the long-tailed porcupine of Southeast Asia (*Trichys fasciculata*) also climbs in trees and shrubs for food. It is the smallest member of the family, weighing less than 4 kg (8.8 pounds), and is somewhat ratlike in appearance; it is about a half metre (1.6 feet) long, not including the tail, which is about half the length of the body. Brush-tailed porcupines (genus *Atherurus*) move swiftly over the ground and can climb, jump, and swim. They sometimes congregate to rest and feed. Brush- and long-tailed species shelter in tree roots, hollow trunks, rocky crevices, termite mounds, caves, abandoned burrows, or eroded cavities along stream banks. Short-tailed porcupines (genus *Hystrix*) are the largest, weighing up to 30 kg (66 pounds), with bodies almost a metre (about 3 feet) long and a tail 8–17 cm (3.1–6.7 inches) long. They move slowly in a ponderous walk but will break into a trot or gallop when alarmed. Like the North American porcupine, they gnaw antlers and bones to supplement their herbivorous diet, which includes the underground portions of plants, fallen fruits, and cultivated crops in addition to bark. Often sheltering in holes, rock crevices, or aardvark burrows, *Hystrix* species also excavate burrows of their own that can become extensive over years of occupation. European populations of the African crested porcupine (*Hystrix cristata*) retreat into their dens during storms and cold spells, but they do not hibernate. This species lives in Italy and Sicily, where it may have been introduced by man, and in Britain, where it was certainly introduced. Old World porcupines bear a litter of one to four (two are usual) after a gestation of approximately 100 days.

Spines of Old World porcupines are flattened, grooved, and flexible or long, hollow, and sharp. *Hystrix* species have large rattle quills on the tail that are large, hollow, and shaped like elongated stemmed goblets. The quills strike each other when the tail is shaken, producing loud sounds used to communicate with other individuals (especially during courtship) and to warn predators. The long quills along head, nape, and back can be erected into a crest. *Atherurus* species also have specialized hollow quills that are used as rattles.

Woodchucks

The woodchuck (*Marmota monax*), which is also called groundhog, is one of 14 species of marmots. It is considered to be a giant North American ground squirrel, and

woodchuck, groundhog, marmot
(*Marmota monax*)

10 cm
4 inches

Woodchuck (Marmota monax). Encyclopædia Britannica, Inc.

it is sometimes destructive to gardens and pasturelands, especially hay, clover, alfalfa, and grass. According to popular legend in the United States, the groundhog emerges from hibernation each year on February 2, designated as Groundhog Day.

This stout-bodied rodent weighs up to 6 kg (13 pounds) and has a body length of up to 50 cm (about 20 inches) and a short, bushy tail up to 18 cm (7.1 inches) long. Thick fur on the upperparts ranges through various shades of brown; the feet are darker and the underparts are buff. Melanistic (nearly black) and albino individuals occur in some populations. Found from the eastern and central United States northward across Canada and into Alaska, they most commonly live along forest edges abutting meadows, open fields, roads, and streams, but they are occasionally encountered in dense forest. The woodchuck is solitary except in the spring, when a litter of four to six young is born (one to nine have been recorded). The young stay with the mother for two to three months.

Although woodchucks dig deep and extensive burrow systems, they are also good swimmers and can climb tall

Woodchuck (Marmota monax). © Photos.com/Jupiterimages

shrubs and sizable trees. They are most active in the morning and the evening, eating grasses and other green plants as well as some fruit and the bark and buds of trees. They feed heavily in summer and early fall, accumulating huge fat reserves for the winter. The animal is a true hibernator. It curls into what appears to be a lifeless ball; its body temperature drops nearly to the ambient temperature of the burrow; and its heart rate decreases from 75 to 4 beats per minute. During the winter months the burrow may also provide shelter for foxes, skunks, opossums, raccoons, and other small animals, particularly cottontail rabbits. Woodchucks were once the objects of sport hunting and are considered quite edible. Classified as a marmot (genus *Marmota*), the woodchuck is a member of the squirrel family, Sciuridae, within the order Rodentia.

CHAPTER 5
EXOTIC RODENTS

While the likes of squirrels, guinea pigs, and hamsters are quite familiar to us, there are those rodent groups that are less well known. Some of these, such as the pacaranas of South America and gundis of Northern Africa, have small geographic distributions. Many of the world's lesser known unusual rodents—such as the hefty capybaras, outgoing viscachas, and the sedentary tuco-tucos—are native to South America. One unusual group, the flying squirrel, occurs in North America and Eurasia.

GENERALLY COMMUNAL FORMS

Several types of exotic rodents form extended family groups, nest in colonies, or develop other communal associations. Colonial species include anomalures, blesmols, degus, chinchillas, and viscachas. In addition, some lemming species collect into large migrating herds during periods when their populations boom.

ANOMALURES

There are seven species of anomalures (family Anomaluridae). This group of African rodents is made up of the large anomalures (genus *Anomalurus*), pygmy anomalures (genus *Idiurus*), and flightless anomalure (genus *Zenkerella*). All live in tropical forests, and the large and pygmy anomalures are the only gliding mammals in Africa.

Anomalures have lightly built skeletons and slender bodies with long limbs and strong, curved claws. The eyes are large, and the fur is dense and silky. Two rows of prominent, overlapping, keeled scales cover the underside of the long tail near its base; the rest of the tail is covered by long hair, which gives it a bushy, tufted appearance. The gliding anomalures have broad, fur-covered membranes formed from skin and muscle. Small membranes extend between the neck and wrists, and larger ones span the tail and hind limbs, but the most expansive are the side membranes connecting the forelimbs and hind limbs. The front part of each side membrane is supported by a cartilaginous strut attached to the elbow joint. This strut differs from a similar structure in flying squirrels that originates from the wrist bones. By extending their limbs, anomalures transform themselves into a gliding platform that they control by manipulating the membranes and tail. The curved claws and tail scales help stabilize the animal when it rests on vertical surfaces.

Large and pygmy anomalures are nocturnal and nest in hollow trees, entering and exiting through holes located at various heights along the trunk. Colonies of up to 100 pygmy anomalures live in some trees. Large anomalures gnaw bark and then lick the exuding sap; they also eat flowers, leaves, nuts, termites, and ants. Pygmy anomalures eat oil palm pulp and insects but also gnaw bark, possibly to obtain sap. A flightless anomalure has been recorded eating termites on a tree trunk, but little else is known about the habits of this rare species.

The largest of the seven species is Pel's anomalure (*A. pelii*), with a body 40 to 46 cm (16 to 18 inches) long and a tail of nearly the same length. The little anomalure (*A. pusillus*) is about half the size of Pel's and has a proportionally shorter tail. The pygmy anomalures (*I. macrotis* and *I. zenkeri*) are smaller still, ranging from 7 to 10 cm (2.8 to 3.9 inches) in body length, not including their long tails (9 to 13 cm [3.5 to 5.1 inches]). The flightless anomalure (*Z. insignis*) is about 20 cm (7.9 inches) long and has a tail slightly shorter than its body.

Though often called scaly-tailed flying or flight-less squirrels, anomalures are not squirrels (family Sciuridae), nor are they even closely related. Rather, family Anomaluridae is classified with spring hares (family Pedetidae) in a separate suborder, Anomaluromorpha. This, however, is an artificial arrangement uniting groups for which evolutionary relationships to other rodents are unknown. In fact, anomalures are not closely related to any living rodents. Their nearest relatives are extinct species, represented only by fossils, that lived in Africa between the Late Eocene (37.2 million to 33.9 million years ago) and Early Pliocene (5.3 million to 3.6 million years ago) epochs.

BLESMOLS

The blesmols (family Bathyergidae) encompass about a dozen species of burrowing African rodents that live in arid regions south of the Sahara (desert). Blesmols are highly adapted to a subterranean lifestyle. They appear virtually neckless, having strong, blunt heads with incisor teeth protruding forward beyond the mouth. The teeth are used for digging, and the mouth can be closed behind the front teeth, which prevents ingestion of soil as the animals dig. Their stocky, cylindrical bodies have short limbs and large feet. The outer borders of the hind feet are fringed with stiff hairs that aid in pushing soil rearward. The forefeet bear small claws, except for the long, strong front claws of the dune blesmols (genus *Bathyergus*). The eyes are very small, and there are no external ears, only openings that are either hidden by fur or surrounded by bare or thickened skin. Blesmols have an acute sense of hearing, however, and they are very sensitive to ground vibrations.

Among the largest of these mole rats are the dune bles-mols (genus *Bathyergus*), which weigh up to 1.8 kg (4 pounds) and are 18 to 33 cm (7.1 to 13 inches) long with very short, hairy tails (4 to 7 cm [1.6 to 2.8 inches]). Smallest is the naked blesmol, more commonly called the naked mole rat (*Heterocephalus glaber*), which weighs 80 grams (2.8 ounces) or less and has a body only 8 to 9 cm (3.1 to 3.5 inches) long and a tail of 3 to 5 cm (1.2 to 2 inches). Its wrinkled skin is pinkish and bald except for a few pale hairs scattered on the body and tail and sparse fringes of hair along the lips and the edges of the feet. The other blesmols have dense, velvety fur of extremely variable colour, ranging from whites and grays through tones of buff and brown to shades of red and black. Many species have a white spot on the head, and some have more extensive white patterns.

Blesmols prefer sandy and loamy soils in dry grasslands and savannas, where they eat roots, bulbs, tubers, other plant parts, and occasionally invertebrates. Most chew through the ground with their incisors to excavate elaborate burrows and use their heads and hind feet to push or kick loosened soil out to the surface into mounds. (Dune blesmols use their front claws and forefeet to dig.) Although blesmols may be active at any time, they rarely, if ever, emerge from their burrows. Dune, cape, and silvery blesmols are solitary, but common and naked mole rats are colonial. Naked mole rats live in underground colonies of up to 300 individuals in arid parts of East Africa. A single breeding female dominates the colony and mates only with a select few males, producing up to five litters per year. All other colony members are nonbreeding or functionally sterile helpers. Litters are the largest of any mammal, numbering up to 27 young, but only about 10 per litter survive to weaning.

The evolutionary history of the blesmol is based upon fossils dating to the Early Miocene Epoch (23 million to 13.8 million years ago) in Africa. One extinct species from the Pleistocene Epoch (2.6 million to 11,700 years ago) was discovered in Israel.

Blesmols are the only members of the family Bathyergidae, with the naked mole rat being assigned its own subfamily (Heterocephalinae) and the other blesmols being members of the subfamily Bathyerginae. The blesmol family belongs to the suborder Hystricognatha within the order Rodentia.

CAPYBARAS

The capybaras (*Hydrochoerus hydrochaeris*), which are also called carpinchos or water hogs, are the largest living rodents. The species is semiaquatic and inhabits Central and South America. The capybara is the sole member of the family Hydrochoeridae, but it resembles the cavy and guinea pig of the family Caviidae.

A capybara and visitor, photographed at the San Diego Children's Zoo, circa 1959. Allan Grant/Time & Life Pictures/Getty Images

South American capybaras may be 1.25 metres (4 feet) long and weigh 66 kg (145 pounds) or more; Panamanian capybaras are smaller and weigh about 27 kg (60 pounds). Capybaras are short-haired, brownish rodents, with blunt snouts, short legs, small ears, and almost no tail. They are shy and associate in groups along the banks of lakes and rivers. They normally feed in the morning and evening and spend most of the day resting under cover along the banks. They are vegetarian and in cultivated areas sometimes become pests by eating melons, grain, and squash. They swim and dive readily and commonly enter water to elude predators such as jaguars and anacondas. Capybaras are edible and in Venezuela are ranched for meat. The female bears a single litter of three to eight young each year; gestation takes about 100 to 110 days.

Cavies

The cavies make up a family (Caviidae) of 14 species of South American rodents. Guinea pigs, maras, yellow-toothed cavies, mountain cavies, and rock cavies are classified in this family. All except the maras have robust bodies, short limbs, large heads and eyes, and short ears. There are four digits on the forefeet but three on the hind feet, and the soles of the feet are hairless. The claws are sharp and the tiny tail is inconspicuous except in the rock cavy, which has blunt claws and a short tail projection. Most cavies are moderately large, weighing 200 to 1,500 grams (0.4 to 3.3 pounds) with a body 15 to 40 cm (6 to 16 inches) long. Their dense, coarse fur ranges from gray to brown on the upperparts and whitish to gray on the underparts.

Maras resemble hares in having large ears and eyes, a blunt muzzle, and long, slender legs. They are larger than the other cavies, weighing 9 to 16 kg (20 to 35 pounds) with a body 45 to 75 cm (17.7 to 29.5 inches) long and a tiny tail of up to 5 cm (2 inches). Their front claws are sharp, but those on the hind feet are hooflike; the dense fur is gray with whitish underparts and has a crisp texture.

Although the rock cavy climbs trees to forage, cavies are terrestrial and colonial. They are active during the day (diurnal) or during early morning and evening (crepuscular). They den at night in burrows that they have excavated or that other mammals have abandoned; some species also find shelter in rock crevices, under brush piles, or in dense vegetation. Their diet is generally any available vegetation, such as grasses, forbs, leaves, and fruit. Even in cold environments, cavies do not hibernate. Breeding seasons vary among species, with gestation periods ranging from 50 to 93 days. Most cavies bear litters of 1 to 4 young, but wild guinea pigs have up to 5 young, and the domestic guinea pig may bear from 1 to 13 young per litter.

Cavies range from Venezuela to southern Patagonia but are not found in western Chile or most of the Amazon River basin. Guinea pigs occupy open grasslands, forest margins, swamps, and rocky areas. The rock cavy dwells among boulders in dry areas of eastern Brazil, whereas yellow-toothed and mountain cavies live in grassy, rocky, and brushy habitats in the Andes Mountains from Peru to Argentina at elevations of up to 4,000 metres (13,000 feet). Maras inhabit the open landscapes of semiarid

Patagonian cavy, or mara (Dolichotis patagona). George Holton—Photo Researchers

grasslands, thorn scrub, and temperate steppes from Bolivia through Argentina and southern Paraguay.

Cavies represent a small segment of an evolutionary history that began in South America during the Middle Miocene Epoch (16.4 million to 11.2 million years ago). Five genera exist today, but fossils of 16 genera have been identified. Caviidae is part of the suborder Hystricognatha within the order Rodentia.

CHINCHILLAS

Both chinchilla species are placed within the genus *Chinchilla*. These medium-sized rodents are native to South America and have been long valued for their extremely soft and thick fur. Once very common, chinchillas were hunted almost to extinction. They remain scarce

Long-tailed chinchilla (Chinchilla laniger). Jane Burton—Bruce Coleman Ltd.

in the wild but are raised commercially and are also sold as housepets. All chinchillas in captivity are descended from 13 animals taken into the United States in 1927.

Chinchillas weigh up to 800 grams (1.8 pounds) with a compact body up to 38 cm (15 inches) long, large eyes, long ears, and a moderately long, bushy tail of up to 15 cm (5.9 inches). Their silky, dense fur is generally bluish to brownish gray except for the yellowish white underparts. Various other colours of chinchilla have been bred in captivity, where they can survive 20 years or more. In their native habitat, chinchillas are colonial, living in arid, rocky environments of the Andes Mountains from southern Peru to Chile at elevations of 800 metres (2,600 feet) near the coast to 6 km (about 4 miles) inland. They usually hide during the day in crevices and cavities among rocks, emerging during the evening and night to feed on any available vegetation. On particularly bright days they occasionally emerge during daylight hours to forage. Following an average gestation period of 111 days, chinchillas usually bear two annual litters of two to three young, although litter sizes from one to six have been recorded.

Both species of *Chinchilla*, the long-tailed chinchilla (*C. laniger*) and the short-tailed chinchilla (*C. brevicaudata*), are protected by law, but poaching and habitat loss continue. Chinchillas and their closest living relatives, the mountain viscachas, along with the more distantly related plains viscacha, constitute the family Chinchillidae of the suborder Hystricognatha within the order Rodentia.

Degus

The degu (genus *Octodon*) is one of four species of ratlike South American rodents found primarily on the lower western slopes of the Andes Mountains. It is one of the most common mammals of central Chile at elevations up to 1,200 metres (3,900 feet), where it prefers open grassy areas near shrubs, rocks, and stone walls.

Degus have a large head, large eyes, and moderate-sized, nearly hairless ears. They weigh 170 to 300 grams (6 to 10.6 ounces) and have a body 25 to 31 cm (9.8 to 12.2 inches) in length and a shorter, black-tipped tail of 8 to 13 cm (3.1 to 5.1 inches). Long, comblike bristles project over claws on the hind feet. The soft, thick fur of the upper-parts is yellowish brown, and there is a pale yellow spot above and below each eye. The underparts are creamy yellow; some individuals exhibit a pale neck band.

Degus are active during the day, especially in the morning and late afternoon. They are colonial and excavate elaborate burrow systems comprising several chambers with main corridors running beneath rocks and shrubs. Near the burrow openings they accumulate piles of sticks, stones, and dung, which may mark territorial boundaries or ownership of nesting sites. Degus travel considerable distances from their burrows to find food. With tail erect, they run to feeding sites through networks of tunnels and along surface paths. Foraging on the ground and also climbing into the branches of shrubs and small trees, degus eat leaves and bark, seeds, green grass, and fruit. They do not hibernate and are active throughout the year, storing food in their burrows for winter. Degu colonies consist of extended family groups. The females bear a litter of 1 to 10 young at least once a year after a gestation period of about three months. Several females in the same social group may raise their young in a common burrow. Adults are known to carry grass to the young in the nest.

The moon-toothed degu (*Octodon lunatus*) lives along coastal Chile, apparently replacing *O. degus* in areas where thicket habitat is common. Bridges's degu (*O. bridgesi*) dwells in forests along the base of the Andes from extreme southern Argentina to central Chile. The Mocha Island degu (*O. pacificus*) is found only in forest habitat on an island off the coast of central Chile; it was not classified as a different species until 1994. Because their habitats are being cleared for agriculture, both the Mocha Island and the Bridges's degu are endangered.

All four degu species belong to the family Octodontidae, a member of the suborder Hystricognatha within the order Rodentia. Their closest relatives are rock rats (genus *Pithanotomys*), viscacha rats (*Octomys*, *Pipanacoctomys*, *Salinoctomys*, and *Tympanoctomys*), the coruro (*Spalacopus*), and the mountain degu, or chozchoz (*Octodontomys*). Tuco-tucos (*Ctenomys*) are in the same family. Octodonts are among some of the earliest South American rodents preserved as fossils, with an evolutionary history extending back to the Late Oligocene Epoch (28.5 million to 23.8 million years ago).

FLYING SQUIRRELS

The subfamily Pteromyinae contains 43 species of gliding squirrels known colloquially as flying squirrels. Two species are North American, two live in northern Eurasia, and all others are found in the temperate and tropical forests of India and Asia. Although these rodents do not fly, glides of up to 450 metres (almost 1,500 feet) have been recorded for Oriental giant flying squirrels (*Petaurista*). Ample, loose skin and underlying muscle typically form a fur-covered membrane between each forelimb and hind limb; some species have smaller membranes between the head and wrists and between the hind limbs and tail. A cartilaginous rod that extends from the wrist supports the front part of each membrane alongside the body.

Flying squirrels are long-limbed and slender and have large eyes; the long, bushy tail may be cylindrical or flattened. Their dense fur is soft and long and either silky or

southern flying squirrel,
North American flying squirrel
(*Glaucomys volans*)

10 cm
4 inches

Southern, or North American, flying squirrel (Glaucomys volans).
Encyclopædia Britannica, Inc.

woolly in texture. A considerable range of body size exists among the 14 genera. Some giant flying squirrels of tropical India and southeastern Asia weigh 1 to 2.5 kg (2.2 to 5.5 pounds) and have a body length of about 30 to 60 cm (12 to 24 inches) and a tail 35 to 64 cm (13.8 to 25.2 inches) long. The smallest are the dwarf flying squirrels (*Petaurillus*) of northern Borneo and the Malay Peninsula; their bodies are just 7 to 9 cm (2.8 to 3.5 inches) long and their tails 6 to 10 cm (2.4 to 3.9 inches). When seen in the tall trees of the tropical rainforest, the glides of these tiny rodents are easily mistaken for the flutter of large butterflies.

Unlike other squirrels, flying squirrels are nocturnal. They den in tree cavities, grottoes or rock crevices on cliffs, and cave ledges. Some also build globular nests high in trees where branches join the trunk. Nests are made of leaves, shredded bark, mosses, or lichens. Most species seldom leave the trees, but North American flying squirrels

(*Glaucomys*) regularly descend to the ground to forage and bury nuts. Depending upon the species, diets can include seeds, fruit, leaves, flower buds, nuts, fungi, lichens, pollen, ferns, tree sap, insects, spiders, other invertebrates, small birds, eggs, snakes, and smaller mammals.

From high in a tree, the squirrel leaps into the air and extends its limbs to stretch the membranes, transforming the body into a gliding platform that is controlled by manipulating the membranes and tail. The animal sails downward to an adjacent tree. Just before the glide ends, it pulls upward, landing deftly on all four feet. When not in use, the membranes are pulled close to the body.

Some authorities regard flying squirrels as a family (Pteromyidae). A few species of anomalure are occasionally called scaly-tailed flying squirrels, but these rodents are classified in the family Anomaluridae. Some researchers have speculated that Pteromyinae is not a single group but members from two different clusters of tree squirrels or possibly nonsquirrel ancestors. Recent evidence derived from fossils and the anatomy of wrist and gliding membranes, however, indicates that all living flying squirrel species are closely related and likely evolved from a tree squirrel ancestor during the Oligocene Epoch (33.7 million to 23.8 million years ago).

GUNDIS

Gundis (family Ctenodactylidae) are North African rodents distinguished by their comblike rows of bristles on the inner two toes of each hindfoot. Each of the five species has a large head, blunt nose, big eyes, and short, rounded ears. The body is 16 to 24 cm (6.3 to 9.4 inches) long, and there is a short, furry tail (1 to 5 cm [0.4 to 2 inches]). Fur is dense, soft, and silky, ranging in colour from gray to pale brown.

Gundis are terrestrial and found only in rocky, sparsely vegetated deserts where the days are long and sunny and the humidity is low for most of the year. Gundis are most active at temperatures between 25 and 30 °C (77 and 86 °F). During the day they are shy, climbing deftly over rocks and sitting on ledges to sunbathe. If the temperature gets too hot, they flatten themselves against cool rock surfaces or retreat to crevices. They do not excavate burrows or build nests but shelter in rocks and caves at night and on cold, wet, or windy days. Gundis groom themselves with their bristled hindfeet. Vocalizations are birdlike, and these sharp whistling calls are emitted upon the approach of predators. Seeds, leaves, flowers, and plant stalks provide gundis with both food and water. No food is stored, and gundis neither accumulate body fat reserves nor hibernate. Breeding occurs in January and April, with one or two young produced after a gestation period of about 55 days.

Common gundis (*Ctenodactylus gundi* and *C. vali*) are found in parts of Morocco, Algeria, Tunisia, and Libya, but the Mzab gundi (*Massoutiera mzabi*) has the largest range, extending from southeastern Algeria through southwestern Libya to northern Mali, Niger, and Chad. The Felou gundi (*Felovia vae*) is confined to Senegal, Mali, and Mauritania. The East African gundi, or Speke's pectinator (*Pectinator spekei*), is geographically isolated from all other gundi species and lives in Ethiopia and Somalia.

Gundis constitute the family Ctenodactylidae (Greek: "comb-toe") and are the only members of the suborder Sciuravida within the order Rodentia. In addition to living gundis, 16 extinct genera of family Ctenodactylidae are represented by fossils from Africa and parts of Asia. Gundis have no close relatives among current rodents, and they form a small relict cluster of an impressive evolutionary diversification that began in the Early Eocene Epoch (54.8 million to 49 million years ago).

HUTIAS

The 26 living, as well as recently extinct, species of hutias (family Capromyidae) are native to the Caribbean region. The surviving species of hutia are short-limbed and stout and have a large head, small eyes and ears, prominent claws, and long whiskers. Size ranges from the rat-sized dwarf hutia (*Mesocapromys nanus*), with a body length of 20 to 30 cm (8 to 12 inches), to the raccoon-sized Desmarest's Cuban hutia (*Capromys pilorides*), with a body 32 to 60 cm (12.6 to 23.6 inches) long and weight of up to 8.5 kg (19 pounds). The tail ranges from very short and inconspicuous in Brown's hutia (*Geocapromys brownii*) to pronounced and prehensile in the long-tailed Cuban hutia (*Mysateles prehensilis*). Depending on the species, the tail may be thinly or thickly furred and have a thick coat of fur that

Bahaman hutia (Geocapromys ingrahami). Painting by H. Douglas Pratt

may be soft or coarse; colours range from gray to brown to black above, with lighter underparts.

Adept tree and rock climbers, most hutias are terrestrial and none are known to burrow. Instead, they den in tree nests and among tree trunk cavities and roots, as well as in deep rock crevices, caves, and holes in limestone. There are diurnal and nocturnal species. The long-tailed Cuban hutias are nocturnal and entirely arboreal and thus rarely descend from tree crowns. They resemble tree squirrels as they run along branches and leap from one tree to another. Hutias eat roots, tubers, leaves, stems, and bark; Desmarest's Cuban hutia also consumes small vertebrates. They obtain all water requirements from their food.

Hunting by native islanders and early European colonists led to the extermination of hutias on various islands. For example, the Puerto Rican hutia (*Isolobodon portoricensis*) was probably indigenous to Hispaniola and introduced to Puerto Rico and some of the Virgin Islands, but it is now extinct. Some hutias are not endangered, but others are rare and becoming more so owing to human population expansion and habitat destruction, especially forests. The remaining populations are found in swamp forests, along coasts, and in rocky, mountainous habitats. Although hutias once ranged from sea level to high elevations, they are presently restricted to cays, steep ravines, or remote mountain valleys.

Hutias constitute the family Capromyidae of the suborder Hystricognatha within the order Rodentia. Their closest living relatives are the nutria and American spiny rats. The oldest species of hutia (genus *Zazamys*) is represented by Cuban fossils from the early Miocene Epoch (23 to 13.8 million years ago). Five species of giant hutia belonging to a separate family, Heptaxodontidae, may have survived into historical time.

LEMMINGS

These small rodents are found only in the Northern Hemisphere. Some of the 20 known species undertake large, swarming migrations. Lemmings have short, stocky bodies with short legs and stumpy tails, a bluntly rounded muzzle, small eyes, and small ears that are nearly hidden in their long, dense, soft fur. The wood lemming (*Myopus schisticolor*) and steppe lemming (*Lagurus lagurus*) are the smallest, measuring 8 to 12 cm (3.1 to 4.7 inches) in body length and weighing 20 to 30 grams (0.7 to 1.0 ounce). The other species are larger, weighing 30 to 112 grams (1.1 to 4 ounces), with bodies 10 to 22 cm (3.9 to 8.7 inches) long. The colour of the collared lemming varies seasonally. During the summer its coat is gray tinged with buff or reddish brown and with dark stripes on the face and back. In the winter they molt into a white coat and develop forked digging claws. Other species are gray, sandy yellow, various tints and tones of brown, or slate gray and black.

Lemmings live throughout temperate and polar regions of North America and Eurasia, inhabiting steppes and semi-deserts, treeless alpine or arctic tundra, sphagnum bogs, coniferous forests, and sagebrush-covered slopes, where they are solitary and generally intolerant of one another. Active year-round, they feed on almost any sort of vegetation, including roots, buds, leaves, twigs, bark, seeds, grasses, sedges, and mosses. Lemmings scamper along extensive runway systems and construct nests in burrows or beneath rocks. Collared and brown lemmings (*Dicrostonyx* and *Lemmus*) make nests on the tundra surface or beneath the snow. Breeding from spring to fall, females can produce up to 13 young after a gestation period of about 20 to 30 days.

Lemmings do not, as is popularly supposed, plunge into the sea in a deliberate suicidal death march. Historically,

Although lemmings usually live on their own or in small groups, sometimes large numbers gather together and move to a new area. Yoshio Otsuka/ Amana Images/Getty Images

collared and brown lemming populations fluctuate dramatically, with highest levels reached every two to five years. After several years of optimal breeding conditions, overutilization of food resources, and low predation, populations become excessively large and more aggressive. As a result, the lemmings may migrate in late summer or fall. Most travel only short distances, but the Norway lemmings (*Lemmus lemmus*) in Scandinavia are a dramatic exception. From a central point, they move in growing numbers outward in all directions, at first erratically and under cover of darkness but later in bold groups that may travel in daylight. Huge hordes overrun broad areas, and some lemmings are often forced to swim water barriers or into human settlements. Many die because they cannot locate a suitable habitat, and others drown when they are pushed into the sea by the pressing momentum of the masses behind them. An especially massive outbreak occurs every 30 to 35 years in Lapland, with the lemmings swarming to central Finland and the Gulf of Bothnia.

Since the mid-1990s, lemming populations in southern Norway have not followed historical patterns. Norway lemmings overwinter in the spaces between the deep snow and the ground surface. Warmer, more humid winters have produced fewer areas of this specialized habitat, and the heavy, wet snow has made remaining spaces less secure.

The 20 lemming species belong to 6 genera, which, along with voles and muskrats, are classified in the subfamily Arvicolinae of the mouse family (Muridae) within the order Rodentia.

NUTRIAS

Nutrias (*Myocastor coypus*), which are also called coypus, are a large amphibious South American rodent with webbed hind feet. The nutria has a robust body, short limbs, small eyes and ears, long whiskers, and a cylindrical, scaly tail. It can weigh up to 17 kg (37.5 pounds), although 5 to 10 kg (11 to 22 pounds) is usual; the body measures up to 70 cm (27.6 inches) long and the tail up to 45 cm (17.7 inches). The yellowish or reddish brown coat contains coarse guard hairs overlying soft, dense underfur.

The nutria is agile on land but is also a superb swimmer that can remain submerged for up to five minutes. It can close its mouth behind the incisor teeth, which allows it to cut submerged vegetation without swallowing water. A wide variety of aquatic vegetation is consumed, including grains, roots, rhizomes, stems, leaves, cattails, water lilies, duckweed, and white clover. Mussels and snails, however, are also part of the diet. Nutrias excavate short or elaborate burrows in riverbanks and lake margins. They also build platform nests in marshes and use floating platforms as feeding sites. Breeding throughout the year, nutrias produce up to three litters of two to eight young annually; gestation takes about 135 days. Activity of these gregarious rodents depends upon season and location; they are nocturnal in most regions but in winter are active during the day.

The nutria's indigenous range extends from southern Brazil and Bolivia southward to Chile and Argentina, where it lives in slow-flowing streams, lakes, and freshwater marshes as well as brackish and saltwater habitats. Because of the fur trade's demand for the nutria's plush underfur, persistent hunting in the 19th and early 20th centuries caused populations to decline. Breeding farms were started in North America and Europe, and some animals escaped or were intentionally introduced into the wild. As a result, feral populations have become established in Canada and at least 15 U.S. states, and substantial populations of nutria in the south-central United States compete aggressively and successfully with the native muskrats. Nutrias are also now widespread in aquatic habitats from England to Central Asia, Japan, and East Africa.

Myocastor coypus is the only living member of the family Myocastoridae in the suborder Hystricognatha within the order Rodentia. Its closest living relatives are degus, American spiny rats, and hutias; some authorities classify the nutria with American spiny rats in the same family (Echimyidae). The nutria is a relict survivor of a diverse group of nine extinct genera represented by fossils from the Early Miocene Epoch (23.8 million to 16.4 million years ago) in southern South America.

Pacaranas

Pacaranas (*Dinomys branickii*) are rare and slow-moving South American rodents found only in tropical forests.

Pacaranas inhabit the western Amazon River basin and adjacent foothills of the Andes Mountains from northwestern Venezuela and Colombia to western Bolivia. It has a chunky body and is large for a rodent, weighing up to 15 kg (33 pounds) and measuring up to 79 cm (31.1 inches) in length, not including the thick, furry tail of up to 20 cm (7.9 inches). The pacarana has a relatively large head with small ears and a thick neck. These parts, along with the forelegs, are essentially solid in colour, but the rest of its coarse black or brown fur is broken by two white stripes grading to spots along the back and rows of white spots on the sides. Very little is known about the animal's natural history in the wild: it is terrestrial but is also a good climber, and it is reported to live in burrows under rocks, eat plant materials, and follow either a diurnal or a nocturnal schedule. In captivity the pacarana is docile and can live for 10 years or more. It has a long gestation period of about 7–8 months, and litter size ranges from one to four young.

The pacarana is the only living member of the family Dinomyidae in the suborder Hystricognatha within the order Rodentia. Containing 22 extinct genera, this family represents a remarkable evolutionary diversification in South America that resulted in some of the largest rodents that ever lived. For example, *Telicomys gigantissimus*, from the Late Miocene Epoch (11.2 million to 5.3 million years ago) of Argentina, was about the size of a small rhinoceros, and another, of the genus *Eumegamys*, matched a hippopotamus in size.

VISCACHAS

Viscachas are a group of four species of slender yet fairly large South American rodents similar to chinchillas. They have short forelimbs, long hindlimbs, and a long, bushy tail. The soft fur is long and dense, and the soles of the feet have fleshy pads.

The three species of mountain viscachas (genus *Lagidium*) live in the Andes Mountains from central Peru southward to Chile and Argentina, usually at altitudes between 4,000 and 5,000 metres (13,000 and 16,000 feet). They have very long ears and resemble long-tailed rabbits. Mountain viscachas weigh up to 3 kg (6.6 pounds) and have a body length of 30 to 45 cm (about 12 to 18 inches). Fur on the upperparts is dark gray to brown, often with a dark stripe down the back; the underparts are white, yellow, or gray. The blackish tail is slightly shorter than the body and is tipped with black or reddish brown. Inhabiting dry, sparsely vegetated rocky cliffs, outcrops, and slopes, these rodents are poor diggers but are agile on the rocks, where they eat grasses, mosses, and lichens. Nonaggressive and

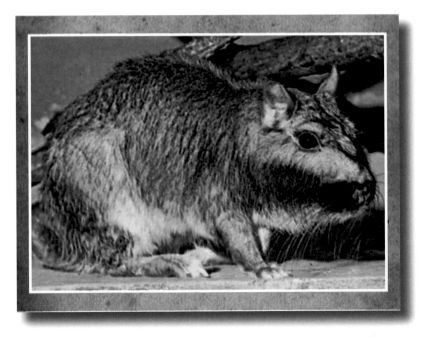

Plains viscacha (Lagostomus maximus). Tom McHugh/Photo Researchers

gregarious, mountain viscachas sometimes form large colonies and spend most of the day among rocks and ledges. The approach of a predator is heralded with loud, abrupt birdlike whistles. At night the viscachas shelter in deep rock crevices and narrow stony tunnels. Females give birth two or three times a year. One young per litter is born after a gestation of about three months.

The plains viscacha (*Lagostomus maximus*) lives on sparse grasslands, or Pampas, in Argentina, Paraguay, and southeastern Bolivia at altitudes up to nearly 3,000 metres (about 9,800 feet). It resembles a huge guinea pig, with a large, blunt head, a body length of 47 to 66 cm (18.5 to 26 inches), and a short tail (15 to 20 cm). Females weigh up to 4.5 kg (9.9 pounds) and males up to 8 kg (17.6 pounds). Coarse guard hairs mingle with soft underfur. Upperparts vary from dark gray to pale brown; underparts are white. Broad black and white stripes—including a moustache— mark the face. There are four large, strong digits on the front feet but only three on the hindfeet. Unlike mountain viscachas, the plains viscacha is nocturnal. It is colonial and digs elaborate burrow systems called *vizcacheras* with its forelegs, pushing the soil away with its nose and marking the entrances with piles of anything it can carry, including sticks, stones, bones, dung, and other objects. Although it will eat any vegetation, seeds and grasses are preferred, which makes the viscacha a pest to ranchers, especially because the burrows are hazardous to both humans and livestock. Plains viscachas are fast and, when pursued, alternate their running with sharp turns and long leaps. Gestation takes about four months, and litters contain one to four young, though two is usual.

Viscachas belong to the family Chinchillidae, a member of the suborder Hystricognatha within the order Rodentia. Mountain viscachas are actually more closely related to chinchillas than they are to the plains viscacha, which is classified in a different subfamily (Lagostominae, rather than Chinchillinae). Extinct ancestors of the plains viscacha are represented by fossils from the Early Miocene Epoch (23.8 million to 20.5 million years ago) in South America; fossil relatives of mountain viscachas and chinchillas have not yet been found.

GROUPS WITH GENERALLY SOLITARY MEMBERS

Although many rodent groups are communal, several contain some species with generally solitary members. For example, the green acouchy (*Myoprocta pratti*) and Azara's agouti (*Dasyprocta azarae*) are solitary during adulthood. Other solitary species include the spring hare (*Pedetes capensis*) and some of the tuco-tucos.

ACOUCHYS

The acouchys (genus *Myoprocta*) are South American rodents that resemble the small tropical-forest-dwelling hoofed animals of Africa and Asia. There are two known species.

    Weighing 1 to 1.5 kg (2.2 to 3.3 pounds), acouchys (which is often incorrectly spelled acouchi or acuchi) are 30 to 39 cm (12 to 15 inches) long, with a very short (4 to 8 cm [1.6 to 3.1 inches]), pencil-thin tail with white hairs on the underside and at the tufted tip. The legs are long and slender, and the three-toed hind feet end in hooflike claws. The coarse fur of the red acouchy (*Myoprocta acouchy*) is dark chestnut red or orange on the sides of the body and legs and black or dark red on the rump; underparts range from dark red to orange. Upperparts of the green acouchy (*M. pratti*) are covered by grizzled fur, each hair of which has several alternating black and yellow bands, giving the animal an overall green or olive-coloured appearance. Underparts are pale orange, sometimes with white patches.

Both species live in mature tropical-lowland rainforest of the Amazon River basin from Colombia, Ecuador, and Peru to western and northern Brazil and the Guianas. Acouchys are terrestrial, active during the day, and usually solitary, bearing litters of one to three young. They eat fruit, seeds, and seedlings and bury nuts in the forest floor throughout their home ranges. Acouchys do not dig shelters but will use cavities constructed by other mammals, particularly armadillo burrows. During the night they rest in leaf nests inside hollow logs on the forest floor. When alarmed, acouchys flee, emitting birdlike whistles and sometimes covering long distances by jumping with both hind feet simultaneously, similarly to the escape behaviour of small African forest antelopes (duikers).

Acouchys are related to agoutis (genus *Dasyprocta*), and both are classified in the family Dasyproctidae of the rodent suborder Hystricognatha. Some authorities assign acouchys to a subfamily (Dasyproctinae) within the agouti family, Agoutidae.

AGOUTIS

Agoutis (genus *Dasyprocta*) encompass about a dozen species of tropical American rodents that resemble the small forest-dwelling hoofed animals of tropical Africa and Asia. Agoutis weigh up to 6 kg (13 pounds), with an elongated body measuring up to 76 cm (2.5 feet) long. They have a large head and rump but slender legs, comparatively small ears, and a tiny, inconspicuous, bald tail. The hind feet have only three toes and hooflike claws. The agouti's coarse, glossy fur ranges from pale orange through shades of brown to blackish, with individual hairs having alternating black and buff bands referred to

Agouti (Dasyprocta). Warren Garst/Tom Stack & Associates

as an agouti pattern. Coloration of the underparts ranges from whitish to buff.

Agoutis are generally wary, and most species are difficult to see or approach in their native habitats. They walk, trot, or gallop on their digits, traveling swiftly when pursued or threatened, and are capable of leaping vertically to 2 metres (6.5 feet) from a standing position. Agoutis are terrestrial, denning at night in burrows among boulders, tree roots, hollow logs, or brushy tangles on the forest floor. Although litters of up to four young have been recorded, two is usual. The agouti's diet consists primarily of fruit, nuts, and seeds, but some species also eat fungi, flowers, leaves, and insects. They bury nuts in the ground for times when food becomes scarce, and, as a result, agoutis are one of the most important mammalian seed dispersers for many species of tropical trees.

Brazilian agouti (Dasyprocta leporina). Encyclopædia Britannica, Inc.

All agouti species are intensively hunted because their flesh is prized as food by indigenous peoples. Agoutis are found from southern Mexico southward to Ecuador and east of the Andes throughout the Amazon River basin. Although most agouti species live in lowland and montane tropical rainforests, Azara's agouti (*Dasyprocta azarae*) also inhabits the drier *cerrado* (savanna and scrub) and *chaco* environments south of the Amazon basin into Paraguay and northeastern Argentina. Three different agoutis have been introduced into the West Indies, presumably by native Caribbean tribes: *D. mexicana* in Cuba, *D. punctata* in Cuba and the Cayman Islands, and *D. leporina*, the Brazilian agouti, in the Virgin Islands and the Lesser Antilles.

Agoutis are closely related to acouchys (genus *Myoprocta*); both are members of the family Dasyproctidae, although some specialists classify dasyproctids as a sub-family (Dasyproctinae) of the family Agoutidae, which also includes pacas. In either case, agoutis are members of the suborder Hystricognatha within the order Rodentia.

Pacas

Pacas (genus *Agouti*) are a South American species with piglike bodies, large heads, and swollen cheeks. Both species have short ears, large eyes, and long whiskers, and their bodies are stout, with large rumps and short limbs. The front feet have four toes, and the hindfeet have five — two tiny side toes and three long, weight-bearing middle toes, all with thick claws.

The paca (*Agouti paca*) is found from southern Mexico to southern Brazil and northern Paraguay, where it lives in tropical forests from sea level to 3,000 metres (9,800 feet). Weighing from 5 to 13 kg (11 to 29 pounds) and having a body 60 to 78 cm (24 to 31 inches) long, it has a stumpy tail (1 to 3 cm [0.4 to 1.2 inches] long) hidden beneath the rump hairs. Straight and bristlelike hairs lie flat in its coarse, shiny coat. The paca's upperparts are dark brown or chestnut, with three or four lines of large white spots extending from head to rump on each side of the body; spots coalesce on some individuals. Underparts are white.

Pacas are most abundant near large rivers, streams, swamps, and dense thickets, but they have also been seen in forests far from water. Terrestrial and monogamous, male and female pacas reside in separate burrows during the day, then at night associate in a small common territory, where they forage independently. Their burrows usually have a main entrance and hidden exits plugged with leaves. Burrows are often dug in dry banks near water. In the limestone terrain of southern Yucatan, pacas do not dig burrows; instead, they den in caves or dry sinkholes.

At night pacas walk heavily and noisily through leaves as they forage along prominent paths for fallen fruit and the occasional plant part or tuber. Sometimes they lie down to rest in the open. When pursued, pacas attempt to escape by heading for water, as they are good swimmers. Females usually bear one, rarely two, well-developed young twice a year after a gestation period of about four months.

Pacas have become scarce or extinct in forests near human settlements, although they are common where not intensively hunted for their tender, veal-like flesh. Their ecological and behavioral traits make them difficult to manage in captivity for meat production, but maintenance of intact forest habitat might result in locally sustainable hunting yields.

The mountain paca (*A. taczanowskii*) is smaller and has a long dense coat. Found high in the Andes Mountains from northwestern Venezuela to Peru, it lives at the upper limits of mountain forest and in alpine pastures.

Pacas are the only members of the family Agoutidae. Their closest living relatives are agoutis and acouchys (family Dasyproctidae). Both families belong to the suborder Hystricognatha, which includes guinea pigs and chinchillas. No paca fossils have been discovered.

SPRING HARES

The spring hare (*Pedetes capensis*), which is also spelled springhare, is a bipedal grazing rodent indigenous to Africa. About the size of a rabbit, the spring hare more closely resembles a giant jerboa in having a short round head, a thick muscular neck, very large eyes, and long, narrow upright ears. Like jerboas, spring hares have short forelegs but long, powerful hind legs and feet used for jumping. Standing on its hind feet and using its tail as a brace, the spring hare moves in a series of short hops with its forefeet held close to the body. When alarmed, it travels quickly in erratic leaps of 2 to 3 metres (6.6 to 9.8 feet) until it reaches a burrow.

Found throughout southern and eastern Africa northward into Kenya, spring hares live in open arid habitats of sandy ground, overgrazed or floodplain grasslands, dry riverbeds, sparse scrub, and cultivated areas. During the day they den in burrows, usually in well-drained, hard-packed sandy soils on flat open land near an abundant source of grass. They dig by using sharp curved claws on the five digits of their forefeet. Large flattened claws on the four digits of the hind feet allow them to throw loosened soil clear of the excavation. Grass is their primary food; they consume all parts of the plant, including roots, but different parts are preferred in different seasons. Spring hares sometimes eat locusts as well as cultivated crops. Litters of one (rarely two) young may be born at any time during the year or, depending on geography, only during the wet season.

Weight generally ranges from 3 to 4 kg (6.6 to 8.8 pounds), and body length is about 35 to 43 cm (14 to 17 inches). The tail is approximately equal in length to the body and is covered with thick hairs that form a

Spring hare (Pedetes capensis). Joel Sartore/National Geographic Image Collection/Getty Images

dark brown or black brush at the tip. The fur is straight, long, soft, and thin, ranging in colour from sandy to reddish brown. The pale fur of the underparts extends to the front of the thighs and inner sides of the legs. A small flap of skin (the tragus) at the base of each ear can be folded back over the ear opening to keep out sand and dust; the nostrils can be closed for the same purpose.

Spring hares are not related to hares and rabbits, which belong to a separate order of mammals (Lagomorpha). Within the order Rodentia, spring hares have been speculatively allied with jerboas (family Dipodidae), gundis (family Ctenodactylidae), African and Asian porcupines (family Hystricidae), or rats and mice (family Muridae). However, most specialists now agree that the spring hare is not closely related to any group of living rodents. The spring hare is the only member of the family Pedetidae, which was recently placed, along with anomalures, in a separate suborder of rodents, Anomaluromorpha. The spring hare's closest relatives are represented only by fossils. The extinct genus *Pedetes* lived in Africa during the Early Pliocene Epoch, probably in habitats similar to those occupied by the living species. A much larger version of the spring hare (genus *Megapedetes*) lived during Miocene times in Asia.

Tuco-Tucos

Tuco-tucos (genus *Ctenomys*) make up a diverse group of South American burrowing rodents that are similar to the North American pocket gopher in both appearance and ecology. There are 48 species, although different authorities recognize from 39 to 56. More continue to be found, reflecting the variability in size, colour, and number of chromosomes among different populations. Their name is derived from the sound they make.

Tuco-tuco (Ctenomys) Painting by H. Douglas Pratt

Tuco-tucos have small eyes, tiny ears, and short muscular legs with strong claws on the digits. Their stout, cylindrical bodies measure up to 25 cm (10 inches) long, with a tail of up to 11 cm (4.3 inches). The dense fur is short in some species and long in others, and it ranges in colour from solid gray through various shades of brown to almost black; underparts are lighter.

Some species are solitary and others colonial, but all tuco-tucos construct extensive burrows that include chambers for nesting and for storage of roots, stems, and grasses. Usually active in early morning and late afternoon, these sedentary rodents remain close to their burrows but will occasionally leave at night to forage. Tuco-tucos breed annually and, depending upon the species, give birth to litters of one to seven well-developed young. Gestation lasts from 102 to 120 days.

Found primarily in the southern half of South America, tuco-tucos have a geographic range that extends from southern Peru and eastern Brazil southward to Tierra del Fuego. They live at elevations ranging from sea level to about 4,000 metres (13,000 feet) in a variety of natural habitats, including Altiplano, tropical forest, and grasslands. Tuco-tucos also live in man-made habitats such as pastures, agricultural fields, and vacant city lots.

Tuco-tucos are members of the degu family (Octodontidae), although they are sometimes classified in their own family (Ctenomyidae). The remarkable array of species is likely due to the sedentary nature of tuco-tucos, which, combined with their burrowing behaviour, results in isolated populations—a condition associated with rapid speciation. All living species appear to have evolved very quickly and recently during the Pleistocene Epoch (2,600,000 to 11,700 years ago).

ZOKORS

Zokors (genus *Myospalax*) make up a group of seven north Asian species of subterranean rodents. They are molelike animals that have chunky cylindrical bodies with short powerful limbs. Their feet are large and robust, and the long front claws are self-sharpening and very strong. The tiny eyes are very sensitive to light and nearly hidden in fur.

Zokors are medium-sized rodents weighing from 150 to 560 grams (about 5 to 20 ounces) and having a body 15 to 27 cm (6 to over 10 inches) long. They are covered in long silky fur, which ranges in colour from grayish to reddish brown or pinkish buff. In one species, white patches adorn the muzzle. The conical tail is short (3 to 10 cm) and scantily haired; it may be uniformly coloured or dark above and white below.

Zokors are vigorous, efficient burrowers. Excavating tunnels with their front feet and claws, they rake loosened soil under themselves, using their incisor teeth to cut obstructing roots. After accumulating a quantity of debris beneath their bodies, the zokors kick it back with the hind feet, then turn around and push the pile through the tunnel and out onto the surface in a mound. The main burrow is dug about 2 metres (6.6 feet) below the surface and is constructed with separate chambers for nesting, food storage, and waste. An extensive network of shallow tunnels passes beneath food plants, and the distribution of surface mounds reflects the animal's underground travels. Zokors do not hibernate but are more active during spring and autumn, bearing one litter of four to six young in the spring. Their diet consists primarily of roots, bulbs, and rhizomes, but they sometimes eat leaves and shoots.

The geographic range of zokors includes northern China, southern Mongolia, and western Siberia. They prefer meadows in wooded regions and along river valleys, particularly mountain valleys at elevations between 900 and 2,200 metres (3,000 and 7,200 feet); sod-covered steppes and stony slopes are avoided. The animal's ideal habitat contains rich dark soil with abundant grasses, tubers, and rhizomes, so it is not surprising that these rodents are also encountered in pastures, abandoned agricultural fields, and vegetable gardens.

Although zokors are often described as "mole rats," moles belong to an unrelated group of mammals (order Insectivora). Nor are zokors closely related to other burrowing rodents, such as African mole rats, bamboo rats, blesmols, blind mole rats, and mole voles. Rather, zokors are a purely north Asian group with no close relatives; they constitute their own subfamily (Myospalacinae) of rodents within the mouse and rat family (Muridae). The fossil history of zokors extends back to the Late Miocene Epoch (11.2 million to 5.3 million years ago) in China.

CHAPTER 6

BATS

Bats (order Chiroptera) are the only mammals capable of flight. This ability, coupled with the ability to navigate at night by using a system of acoustic orientation (echolocation), has made the bats a highly diverse and populous order. More than 1,100 species are currently recognized, and many are enormously abundant. Observers have concluded, for example, that some 100 million female Mexican free-tailed bats (*Tadarida brasiliensis mexicana*) form summer nursery colonies in Texas, where they produce about 100 million young in five large caves. The adult males are equal in number to the females, though they do not all range as far north as Texas. Furthermore, this species is found throughout tropical America. Thus, one species alone numbers, at the very least, in the hundreds of millions.

GENERAL FEATURES

All bats have a generally similar appearance in flight, dominated by the expanse of the wings, but they vary considerably in size. The order is usually divided into two well-defined suborders: the Megachiroptera (the large Old World fruit bats) and the Microchiroptera (small bats found worldwide). Among members of the Megachiroptera, flying foxes (*Pteropus*) have a wingspan of 1.5 metres (about 5 feet) and a weight of 1 kg (2.2 pounds). The largest insectivorous bat is probably the naked, or hairless, bat (*Cheiromeles torquatus*); it weighs about 250 grams (about 9 ounces). The largest of the carnivorous bats (and the largest bat in the New World) is the spectral bat (*Vampyrum spectrum*), also known as the tropical American false vampire bat, with a wingspan of over 60 cm (24 inches). The tiny hog-nosed, or bumblebee, bat (*Craseonycteris thonglongyai*) of Thailand is one of the smallest mammals. It has a wingspan of barely 15 cm (6 inches) and weighs about 2 grams (about 0.07 ounce).

Bats vary in colour and in fur texture. Facial appearance, dominated by the muzzle and ears, varies strikingly between families and often between genera. In several families a complex fleshy adornment called the nose leaf surrounds the nostrils. Although the exact function of these facial appurtenances has yet to be determined, scientists believe they may help to direct outgoing echolocation calls. Wing proportions are modified according to mode of flight. The tail and the membrane between the legs also differ, perhaps as adaptations to feeding, flight, and roosting habits. Finally, bats vary in the postures they assume when roosting, particularly in whether they hang suspended or cling to a wall and in the manner in which the wings are folded and used.

DISTRIBUTION

Bats are particularly abundant in the tropics. In West Africa, for example, 31 genera embracing 97 species have been cataloged; in the United States 19 genera, totaling 45 species, are known. Of the 18 bat families, 3—the vesper bats (family Vespertilionidae), free-tailed bats (family Molossidae), and horseshoe bats (family Rhinolophidae)—are well represented in the temperate zones. A few American leaf-nosed bats (family Phyllostomidae) range into mild temperate regions. Several vesper bats range well into Canada.

The Vespertilionidae are found worldwide except in the polar regions and on isolated islands. The brown bats of genus *Myotis* have a range almost equal to that of the entire order. The free-tailed bats and sheath-tailed bats (family Emballonuridae) also encircle the Earth but are restricted to the tropics and subtropics. The horseshoe bats extend throughout the Old World, the round-leaf bats (family Hipposideridae) and Old World fruit bats (family Pteropodidae) throughout the Old World tropics, and the leaf-nosed bats throughout the New World tropics and slightly beyond. The other families have more restricted ranges.

IMPORTANCE TO HUMANS

Most bats are insectivorous, and they are important to humans primarily for their predation on insects, for pollination, and for seed dispersal. Little is known of the spectrum of insect species consumed, but the sheer quantity is formidable. The Mexican free-tailed bats of Texas have been estimated to consume about 9,100 metric tons (10,000 tons) of insects per year. Bats would thus seem to be important in the balance of insect populations and possibly in the control of insect pests.

Some bats feed on pollen and nectar and are the principal or exclusive pollinators of a number of tropical and subtropical plants. Others feed on fruit and aid in dispersing seeds, although bananas and figs must in some cases be protected from fruit-eating bats by early harvest or by nets.

Vampire bats (family Phyllostomidae, subfamily Desmodontinae) are considered serious pests of livestock in some parts of tropical America because the small wounds they cause provide egg-laying sites for parasites and because the vampires may transmit rabies and trypanosomiasis to cattle. Other bats also carry rabies or related viruses.

The guano (droppings) of insectivorous bats is still used for agricultural fertilizer in many countries and in the past was used as a source of nitrogen and phosphorus munitions. Large guano deposits, in addition, cover and thus preserve many archaeologically interesting artifacts and fossils in caves.

In tropical regions large colonies of bats often inhabit houses and public buildings, where they attract attention because of their noisiness, guano, and collective odour. In western culture bats have been the subject of unfavourable myths; in parts of the Orient, however, these animals serve as symbols of good luck, long life, and happiness. In some parts of Southeast Asia and on some Pacific islands, flying foxes (*Pteropus*) are hunted for food. Small bats are also widely but irregularly eaten.

Certain physiological aspects of some bats, particularly those involving adaptations for long hibernation, daily lethargy, complex temperature regulation, acoustical orientation, and long-distance migrations, are of interest to biologists.

In species and numbers, bats constitute an important and generally nonintrusive form of wildlife. Several zoos have established interesting exhibits of bats; indeed, some flying foxes and fruit bats have been exhibited in European zoos since the mid-19th century, and they have been kept widely for research purposes. Bats are interesting pets but require specialized care.

NATURAL HISTORY

Bats are largely known for their nocturnal habits, but they also engage in specialized locomotive and roosting behaviours. One group, the microchiropterans (suborder Microchiroptera), uses echolocation to guide

its movement through obstacles. Most bat pairs produce one offspring, and the adults of many species are
long-lived.

BEHAVIOUR

Nocturnal activity is a major feature of the behavioral
pattern of bats: nearly all species roost during the day
and forage at night. Carnivorous bats, vampire bats, and
perhaps fishing bats may have an advantage at night over
inactive or sleeping prey. In addition, nocturnal flight
protects bats from visual predators, exposure to the sun,
high ambient temperature, and low relative humidity. The
large area of naked wing skin might mean that bats would
absorb rather than radiate heat if they were active during
the day. They would also lose body water required for temperature regulation and would then be forced to forage
near water or somehow retain more water (and thus more
weight) in their bodies during flight.

The nocturnal activity pattern in bats is probably kept
in synchrony with changing day lengths by their exposure
to light at dusk or dawn. Bats often awaken and fly from
the cave exit well before nightfall. Should they be too
early, their internal clock may be reset. A few species of
bats, including a flying fox (*Pteropus samoensis*), the yellow-
winged bat (*Lavia frons*), and the greater sac-winged bat
(*Saccopteryx bilineata*), may forage actively during the day,
but little is yet known of their special adaptations.

In addition to their nocturnal preferences, bats engage
in other notable behaviours. Although they are known
for their flight ability, bats use their claws to shift from
one position to another when hanging upside down, and
various species possess the ability to crawl, walk, and even
leap. Most species form colonial roosts in habitats with

special requirements. Microchiropteran bats use echo-location to guide their movements. Many species target flying insects as their prey. Some species also feed on other arthropods (spiders, scorpions, etc.), fish and crustaceans, or fruit. Bats also groom themselves and interact socially with one another.

Locomotion

Flight is the primary mode of locomotion in all bats, although flight styles vary. Some groups (the free-tailed bats, for example) are adapted for flight in open spaces and high altitudes. They have long, narrow wings, swift flight, and a large turning radius. Slit-faced bats (Nycteridae), false vampire bats (Megadermatidae), and others are adapted for hovering as they pick prey off vegetation or feed on flowers. These bats have short, broad wings, slow flight, and a small turning radius. Some bats take flight easily from the ground: members of the genus *Macrotus* do so simply by flapping, while vampire bats (*Desmodus*) leap into the air and then spread their wings and fly. The free-tails, however, roost well above the ground because, upon takeoff, they fall before becoming airborne.

Though flight speeds in the wild are hard to measure, four vesper bat species, carefully observed, have been timed on average at 18.7 to 33.3 km (11.7 to 20.8 miles) per hour. In flight the posture of each of the four fingers incorporated into the wing is under precise and individual control. Finger and arm postures, which determine the shape, extension, and angle of the wings, govern such actions as turning, diving, landing, and hovering. Except when interrupted by insect catches or obstacles, bat flight paths are straight. Insects may be pursued and captured at a rate of up to two per second; during each catch the flight path is interrupted and thus appears erratic.

BAT-LOVING FLOWERS: CHIROPTEROPHILOUS PLANTS

More than 500 species of tropical plants are pollinated by nectar- and pollen-eating bats, and they have evolved special features to make their nectar and pollen attractive to the nocturnal flyers. Such plants are called chiropterophilous, or "bat-loving" (bats being mammals of the order Chiroptera). Plants that rely primarily on bat pollinators cater to them with large, white flowers, which bats can spot easily at night. The flowers often have a fermented or musky odour, and they tend to open after sunset, just as bats leave their day roosts to feed. In order to accommodate a bat's face, many bat-pollinated flowers are shaped like a vase, although some are flat and brushy in order to load a bat's whiskers with pollen.

Chiropterophilous plants even manufacture substances that are useless to the plant itself but helpful to the bat. Because bats often eat the pollen as well as the nectar of their flowers, the pollen of bat-loving plants is high in protein and contains two amino acids, tyrosine and proline, that are crucial to bat health. Proline is important in building strong wing and tail membranes, and tyrosine is essential for milk production.

Nectar-eating bats (of which there are more than 30 genera) have special adaptations also. They tend to have fleshy bristles on their long tongues, as do many bees, to scoop out pollen as well as nectar. They have good eyesight and a fine sense of smell; often their sonar is reduced. Migratory bats pollinate a variety of species as they travel, and plants are often seen to flower in sequence along a sort of "nectar corridor" corresponding to the bats' migratory route.

In many cases there is little locomotion other than flight. Bats that hang in caves may move across the ceiling by shifting their toehold, one foot at a time. A few genera, especially among the Old World fruit bats (family Pteropodidae), may crawl along branches in a slothlike posture, using their thumb claws as well as their feet. The sheath-tailed bats (family Emballonuridae) and mouse-tailed bats (family Rhinopomatidae) hang on vertical surfaces suspended by their hind claws but with their thumbs and wrists propped against the surface. In this orientation they can scramble rapidly up or down and forward or backward, as well as sideways.

Bats of many families walk or crawl on either horizontal or vertical surfaces, using hind feet, wrists, and thumbs. Many move freely either backward or forward, a convenience for entering and leaving crevices. The vampire bats may also leap from roost to roost. The disk-winged bats (family Thyropteridae) and sucker-footed bat (one species, family Myzopodidae), as well as the bamboo bats (*Tylonycteris*), have specialized wrist and sole pads for moving along and roosting on the smooth surface of leaves or bamboo stalks. Bats are not known to swim in nature except, perhaps, by accident. When they do fall into water, however, they generally swim competently.

ROOSTING

Bats choose a variety of diurnal roosts, although the roost requirements of many bats, which are rather precise in terms of light, temperature, and humidity, limit their distribution. Each species favours a particular kind of roost, though this varies with sex, season, and reproductive activity. Many bats prefer isolated or secure roosts — caves, crevices in cliff faces, the interstices of boulder heaps, tree hollows, animal burrows, sewers, abandoned buildings, portions of buildings inaccessible to humans or infrequently accessed by them (i.e., a roof, attic, or hollow wall), or the hollow core of bamboo stalks. Some species roost externally—on tree trunks or in the branches of trees, under palm leaves, in unopened tubular leaves, or on the surface of rocks or buildings. For some the darkness, stability of temperature and humidity, and isolation from

Indiana brown bats (Myotis sodalis) *hibernating on a cave ceiling.* Allan Roberts

predators provided by caves and crevices seem essential. Others prefer the heat and dryness of sun-exposed roosts. Many bats also occupy nocturnal roosts, often rocky overhangs or cave entrances, for napping, for chewing food, or for shelter from bad weather. Many species likewise choose special nursery or hibernation roosts. Buildings are so widely exploited by bats (especially vesper bats, free-tailed bats, and sheath-tailed bats) that many species have probably become more abundant since the advent of architecture.

Bats are usually colonial; indeed, some form very large cave colonies. Generally, large colonies are formed by bats that roost in dense clusters, pressing against one another, although many are widely spaced and do not touch when roosting. Some of the Old World fruit bats strikingly defoliate the trees on which they roost. In trees flying foxes (*Pteropus*) may form outdoor camps numbering hundreds of thousands of individuals. Many species form smaller groups of several dozen to several hundred. Less commonly, bats are solitary; sometimes the adult female roosts only with its most recent offspring. Occasionally, one sex is colonial and the other is apparently solitary. The advantages of colonial or solitary life and the factors that govern colony size in bats with colonial predilection have not yet been established.

Elaborate communities of other animals are often satellites of cave-bat colonies. Among these are cave crickets, roaches, blood-sucking bugs, a variety of parasites (e.g., fleas, lice, ticks, mites, and certain flies), and dermestid beetles and other insects that feed on cave-floor debris—guano, bat and insect corpses, and discarded pieces of food or seeds. Molds and other fungi are also conspicuous members of the cave-floor community. Bats and their excretions alter the cave environment by producing heat, carbon dioxide, and ammonia.

Migration

Many bats of temperate climates migrate annually to and from summer roosts and winter hibernation sites, with an individual often occupying the same roosts in seasonal sequence each year. Members of the same species may converge on a single hibernation cave or nursery roost from many directions, which indicates that the choice of migration direction to and from these caves cannot be genetically determined. When migration occurs, however, is probably genetically determined (i.e., instinctive) and influenced also by weather conditions and the availability of food. Nothing is known of how bats recognize migration goals or how succeeding generations learn their locations.

Female young born at a nursery roost may memorize its location, but how they know where to go at other times is not clear. Likewise, little is yet known of energy storage, navigation, or other specializations for migrations.

Female Mexican free-tailed bats migrate from central Mexico to Texas and adjacent states each spring, returning south in the fall. Mating probably occurs in transient roosts during the spring flight. The migration is believed to remove pregnant and lactating females to a region of high food supply where they need not compete with males of their own species. Presumably they return to Mexico for its suitable winter climate and food supply and to meet their mates.

The North American red and hoary bats (*Lasiurus borealis* and *L. cinereus*) and the silver-haired bat (*Lasionycteris noctivagans*) migrate in the fall from the northern United States and Canada to the southern United States and beyond, returning in the spring.

ORIENTATION

Bats of the suborder Microchiroptera orient acoustically by echolocation ("sonar"). They emit short high-frequency pulses of sound (usually well above the range of human hearing) and listen to the echoes returning from objects in the vicinity. By interpreting returning echoes, bats may identify the direction, distance, velocity, and some aspects of the size or nature (or both) of objects that draw their attention. Echolocation is used to locate and track flying and terrestrial prey, to avoid obstacles, and possibly to regulate altitude; orientation pulses may also serve as communication signals between bats of the same species. Rousette bats (megachiropteran genus *Rousettus*) have independently evolved a parallel echolocation system for obstacle avoidance alone. Echolocation pulses are produced by vibrating membranes in the larynx and emitted via the nose or the mouth, depending upon species. Nose leaves in some species may serve to channel the sound.

The echolocation signals spread in three dimensions on emission, the bulk of the energy in the hemisphere in front of the bat or in a cone-shaped region from the nostrils or mouth. When the sound impinges on an intervening surface (an insect or a leaf, for example), some of the energy in the signal is reflected or scattered, some absorbed, and some transmitted and reradiated on the far side of the surface; the proportion of sound energy in each category is a function of wavelength and of the dimensions, characteristics, and orientation of the object. The reflected sound spreads in three dimensions, and some portion of it may impinge on the bat's ears at perceptible energy levels.

Bats' external ears are generally large, which probably enhances their value for detecting the direction of incoming signals, and their middle and inner ears are specialized for high-frequency sensitivity. In addition, the bony otic (auditory) complex is often isolated acoustically from the skull, which probably improves signal comparison by both ears. The thresholds and ranges of hearing in several genera of bats have been studied, and in each case the region of maximum sensitivity has been found to coincide with the prominent frequencies of the outgoing echolocation signals.

The characteristics of echolocation pulses vary with family and even with species. Echolocation pulses of a substantial number of bat species have been analyzed in terms of frequency, frequency pattern, duration, repetition rate, intensity, and direction. The prominent frequency or frequencies range from 12 kilohertz (1 kilohertz is equivalent to 1,000 hertz, or cycles per second) to about 150 kilohertz or more. Factors influencing frequency may include bat size, prey size, the energetics of sound production, inefficiency of the propagation of high frequencies, and ambient noise levels.

Orientation pulses may be of several types. The individual pulse may include a frequency drop from beginning to end (frequency modulation [FM]), or the frequency may be constant (CF) during part of the pulse, followed by a brief FM sweep; either FM or CF pulses may have high harmonic content. The pulse duration varies with the species and the situation. During cruising flight the pulses of the greater false vampire bat (*Megaderma lyra*) are 1.5 milliseconds (0.0015 second), those of Wagner's mustached bat (*Pteronotus personatus*) 4 milliseconds, and those of the greater horseshoe bat (*Rhinolophus ferrumequinum*) 55–65 milliseconds. In goal-oriented flight, such as the pursuit of an insect or the evaluation of an obstacle or a landing perch, the pulse duration is systematically altered (usually shortened) with target distance, sometimes ending with pulses as short as 0.25 millisecond.

During insect pursuit, obstacle avoidance, and landing maneuvers, there are three phases of pulse output design: search, approach, and terminal. The search phase, during which many bats emit about 10 pulses per second, precedes specific attention to a target. In the approach phase, which starts when the bat detects an object to which it subsequently devotes its attention, the bat raises the pulse rate to about 25 to 50 per second, shortens the pulses with decreasing distance, and often alters the frequency pattern. The terminal phase, which often lasts about 100 milliseconds, is characterized by extremely short pulses, repeated as rapidly as 200 or more times per second, and ceases as the bat intercepts the target or passes it (the stimulus being, perhaps, the cessation of echoes); another search phase follows. During the brief terminal phase (a fraction of a second), the bat is engaged in final interception (or avoidance) maneuvers and appears to pay little attention to other objects.

In addition to sensitive ears, the use of echolocation to gain sensory information requires integration of the vocal and auditory centres of the brain. Not only must the nervous system of the bat analyze in a few thousandths of a second the reflected, and thus altered, form of its own pulse, but it must separate this echo from those of other individuals and from others of its own pulses. All of this must be done while the animal (and often the target) is moving in space. In the laboratory, bats have been found to be able to identify, pursue, and capture as many as two fruit flies (*Drosophila*, about 3 mm [0.12 inch] long) per second and to locate and avoid wires as fine as 0.1 or even 0.08 mm (0.004 or 0.003 inch) in diameter.

Research has provided some information on the mechanisms of bat sonar. There is evidence that the multiple frequencies of FM or harmonic patterns serve in determining target direction. The relative intensities of the various frequencies are different at each ear, which allows the animal to determine the target's direction when three or more frequencies are received. Target velocity may be measured by CF bats through the use of what is called the Doppler shift, a change in perceived frequency due to the relative motion of the bat and its target. Changes in pulse-echo timing may provide information on target distance and velocity. The ratio of useful signal to background noise is increased by several mechanisms, including specializations of the middle ear and its ossicles (tiny bones), isolation of the cochlea (the area where sound energy is converted into nerve impulses), and adaptations of the central nervous system.

PRESTIN

In microchiropteran bats and some toothed whales, a mutated form of a protein called prestin increases their sensitivity to high-frequency sounds and thereby facilitates the detection of return echos. The nearly identical molecular structure of the *Prestin* gene in these animals, which differs from the structure of the *Prestin* gene found in all other mammals, is an example of convergent evolution, in which the two groups independently evolved the same form of the echolocating protein in response to similar environmental pressures.

Food Habits

Most bats feed on flying insects. In some cases prey species have been identified from stomach contents or from discarded pieces under night roosts, but such studies have not yet provided an adequate measure of the spectrum of bat diets. Bats identify and track insects in flight by echolocation. Large insects may be intercepted with the wing membranes and pulled into the mouth. Some bats feed on arthropods, such as large insects, spiders, and scorpions, that they find on the ground, on walls, or on vegetation. These bats may either land on and kill their prey before taking off with it or pick it up with their teeth while hovering.

Two genera (*Noctilio* and *Myotis*) include at least one species that catches small fish and possibly crustaceans. All fish-eating species also feed on flying insects or have close relatives that do so. Each is specialized in having exceptionally large hind feet armed with long, strong claws with which the fish are gaffed.

The Megachiroptera and many of the phyllostomid genera feed on a variety of fruits, often green or brown in colour; usually such fruits are either borne directly on

D'Orbigny's round-eared bat (Tonatia silvicola) *capturing a katydid in flight.* © Merlin D. Tuttle, Bat Conservation International/Photo Researchers, Inc.

wood or hang well away from the bulk of the tree and have a sour or musky odour.

The Old World fruit bat subfamily Macroglossinae (and some other fruit bats) and certain leaf-nosed bats feed, at least in part, on nectar and pollen. Many tropical flowers, adapted for pollination by these bats, open at night, are white or inconspicuous, have a sour, rancid, or mammalian odour, and are borne on wood, on pendulous branches, or beyond or above the bulk of the plant. The phyllostomid Glossophaginae may also feed on flowers.

Several phyllostomid and megadermatid genera are carnivorous, feeding on small rodents, shrews, sleeping birds, tree frogs, lizards, and other bats. The true vampires, which feed on the blood of large mammals or birds, land near a quiet prospective victim, walk or jump to a vulnerable spot on it where the skin is relatively exposed—the edge of the ear or nostril, around the anus, or between the toes, for example—make a scooping, superficial bite from which the blood oozes freely, and lap the blood with very specialized tongue movements. Each vampire requires about 15 millilitres (roughly half an ounce) of blood per night.

The interaction of bats with their food, be it insects, fruit, or flowers, probably has a substantial impact on some biological communities. Many plants are dependent on bats for pollination; other plants benefit from seed dispersal by bats. Moths of two families are known to take evasive or protective action on hearing bat pulses nearby, an adaptation that implies heavy predation.

MAINTENANCE BEHAVIOUR

Bats are meticulous in their grooming, spending a fair part of the day and night combing their fur and cleansing their wing membranes. Generally, they comb with the claws of one foot while hanging by the other; they remove the combings and moisten their claws with their lips and tongue. On the wing membranes in particular, bats use the mouth meticulously, perhaps oiling the skin with the secretions of dermal (skin) glands while cleansing it.

SOCIAL INTERACTIONS

Although social interactions per se have not been observed between adult bats, they are known to often segregate by sex. As noted earlier, pregnant females in many species occupy special nursery roosts until their young are independent. In some species the sexes occupy the same general roost but gather in separate clusters. In others the sexes intermingle or arrange themselves into a pattern within a group—the females centrally, for example, and the males peripherally. Sexual segregation during foraging has been reported for several species. Among bats that migrate over long distances, such as Mexican free-tailed, red, and hoary bats, the sexes may meet only briefly each year.

LIFE CYCLE

Details of the life cycle are known for only a few species. In northern temperate zone species, there is an annual cycle of sexual activity, with birth taking place between May and July. In males the testes, normally located in the abdominal region, descend seasonally into the scrotum (external pouch), and active spermatogenesis occurs. In females sexual receptivity may be associated with egg maturation and release. Tropical bats may exhibit a single annual sexual cycle or may be diestrous (i.e., have two periods of fertility) or polyestrous (have many).

The sexual cycles of entire populations are closely synchronized, so almost all mating occurs within a few weeks. The periods of gestation, birth, lactation, and weaning are also usually synchronized. Gestation varies in duration: five or six months in flying foxes (*Pteropus*), more than five months in vampire bats (*Desmodus*), three months in some small leaf-nosed bats (*Hipposideros*), and 6 or 7 to 14 weeks in several small vesper bats (family Vespertilionidae). The length of gestation may be influenced by both ambient (surrounding) and body temperature.

In several North American and northern Eurasian vesper and horseshoe bats that hibernate, copulation occurs in the fall, and the sperm are stored in the female genital tract until spring. Ovulation, fertilization, and implantation occur after emergence from hibernation, when the female again has available an abundant food supply and a warm roost. Such favourable environmental conditions greatly enhance the young bat's chances of survival.

Most bats bear one young, but the big brown bat (*Eptesicus fuscus*) may bear twins, and the Eastern red bat (*Lasiurus borealis*) bears litters of one to four.

At birth the young, which may weigh from one-sixth to one-third as much as the mother, usually have well-developed hind legs with which they hold on to their mother or to the roost. Their wings are very immature. The young are hairless or lightly furred and are often briefly blind and deaf. Female bats normally have one pectoral (at the chest) or axillary (at the armpit) mammary gland on each side. Several species that carry their young while foraging also have a pair of false pubic nipples, which the infant may hold in its mouth when its mother flies. The infants are nourished by milk for a period of about five or six weeks in many small bats and for five months in the Indian flying fox (*Pteropus giganteus*). By two months of age, most smaller bats have been flying and foraging for three or four weeks and have achieved adult size.

In many species females late in pregnancy migrate to special nursery roosts, in which large numbers of pregnant females may aggregate, usually to the exclusion of non-pregnant females, males, and bats of other species. In some cases the nursery roosts seem to be chosen for their high temperature, which may derive from the sun, from the bats themselves, or from decomposing guano. When foraging, some bats (*Erophylla*) leave their infants hanging quietly, one by one, on the cave wall or ceiling. In the case of the Mexican free-tailed bat and a few others, the closely spaced infants may move about and mingle on the wall. Some bats carry their young with them for a short period of time. Generally, each mother, on returning to her roost, seeks out her own offspring by position, smell, and acoustical exchange.

Some bats achieve sexual maturity in their first year, others in their second. Infant mortality appears to be high. Developmental and genetic errors and disease take their toll, but accidents seem to cause more serious losses — the young may fall from the ceiling or perhaps have serious collisions in early flight attempts. A fair number of bats probably fail to make the transition from dependent infants to self-sufficient foragers.

Adult bats, on the other hand, have low mortality. Predation is rarely serious, especially for cave-dwelling species. Disease, parasitic infestation, starvation, and accidents apparently take small tolls. There are records of several big brown (*Eptesicus fuscus*), little brown (*Myotis lucifugus*), and greater horseshoe bats (*Rhinolophus ferrumequinum*) that have lived more than 20 years, and a few have lived more than 30. Probably many bats in temperate climates live more than 10 years. Longevity has not been established for most tropical species, but a few are known to live for more than 10 years.

Several factors probably contribute to the unusual longevity of bats. Generally isolated roosts and nocturnal flight substantially protect them from predation, from some elements of weather, and from exposure to the sun. Their largely colonial way of life may ensure that entire populations experience contagious infection and subsequent immunity; indeed, such a pattern in the past may have hastened adaptation to disease. The persistent use of various seasonal roosts probably ensures isolation and security, food and water supplies, and access to mates. Many bats, moreover, reduce their body temperature at rest. Not only is there a probability that this conserves some cellular "machinery," since metabolism is reduced, but fewer hours need to be spent in actively seeking food and water.

FORM AND FUNCTION

Bats are mammals with front limbs modified for flight. The chest and shoulders are large and well-muscled to provide power to the wings. The hips and legs are slender, as they do not usually support any body weight. Wing shape, governed by the relative lengths of the forearm and the fingers, varies greatly, in adaptation to flight characteristics. The fingers, other than the thumb, are greatly elongated and are joined by a membrane that extends from the posterior border of the forearm and upper arm to the side of the body and leg as far as the ankle or foot. The wing membrane consists of two layers of skin, generally darkly pigmented and hairless, between which course blood

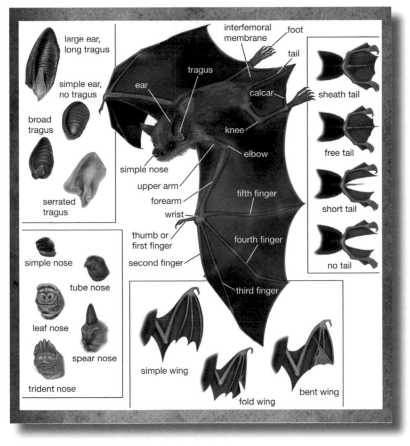

Features of typical microchiropteran bats. Encyclopaedia Britannica, Inc.

vessels and nerves. When not fully extended, the wing skin is gathered into wrinkled folds by elastic connective tissue and muscle fibres. Some of the fingers, especially the third, fold over when the bat is not in flight; the wing may then be quite tightly folded or may partly enfold the bat's undersurface. The thumb, always free of the wing membrane, is used for walking or climbing in some species; in others it is used for handling food. Only the thumb—and occasionally the index finger—ends with a claw. Bats that walk often have pads or suction disks on their thumbs or wrists or both, and many female bats use their thumbs to suspend themselves, hammock fashion, when giving birth.

Most bats have a membrane, consisting of skin like that of the wings, that extends between their legs (the uropatagium, or interfemoral membrane). In the midline the interfemoral membrane is usually supported, at least in part, by the tail, with the edges often shaped in flight by greatly elongated heel bones, or calcars. The interfemoral membrane, especially well-developed in insectivorous, carnivorous, and fish-eating bats, is less-well-developed or even absent in the vampires and in fruit- and flower-feeding bats. Many bats, on catching large prey in flight, bring the membrane forward and, by flexing the neck and back, tuck the prey against and into the membrane. With this maneuver the bat takes hold of the victim headfirst and is able to kill or disable it promptly.

At rest a bat's head, especially the ears, is its most striking feature. The neck is likely to be short and relatively immobile. The projecting portion of the external ear (the pinna) is usually extremely large and often is funnel-shaped. In several genera that feed on terrestrial arthropods, the ears are particularly oversized, probably for highly precise directional assessment. A projection on the front side of the auditory canal (the tragus) or another on the rear side (antitragus) may also be conspicuous. The ears are often highly mobile, sometimes flicking back and forth in phase with the production of sonar signals. In some species the ears are immobile, but in all cases they probably function in tandem for directional analysis.

Bats often have a rodentlike or foxlike muzzle, but in many the face has a pushed-in puglike appearance. In the nectar feeders the snout is elongated to house the long extensible tongue. Many bats have a facial ornament, the nose leaf, which consists of skin and connective tissue. It surrounds the nostrils and extends as a free flap or flaps above the nostrils and in front of the face. The complexity and shape of the nose leaf varies with family; its presence correlates with nasal emission of orientation signals. Thus, it is supposed that the nose leaf influences sound output, perhaps by narrowing the beam, but evidence is sparse.

Most bats are well furred except for the wing membranes. Colours are generally shades of brown, tan, gray, or black on top and lighter shades on the underside. Red, yellow, or orange variants occur in many species. Speckled or mottled patterns are common, as are bright or light-coloured spots or stripes. Bright red, yellow, or orange shading on the head, neck, and shoulders is not unusual. Mottled fur may enable the bat to be inconspicuous on lichen-covered bark or rock. Bright spots may simulate the speckled sunlight of the forest canopy as seen from below. Stripes probably break up contours. The colouring seen while the animal is hanging may be a kind of countershading for concealment, or it may enhance the bat's simulation of a ripening fruit or a dead leaf. Many bats that roost externally hang from a branch by one foot, which then looks like a plant stem.

Many bats have large dermal glands, the location of which depends on family. These glands secrete odorous substances that may serve as species or sex recognition signals (pheromones). Some glands may also supply oils for conditioning the skin or waterproofing the fur.

HIPPOSIDERINAE

Hipposiderinae is a subfamily of insect-eating bats, suborder Microchiroptera, family Rhinolophidae, with 9 genera and approximately 66 species. Known as roundleaf bats, hipposiderine bats are characterized by a round nose leaf (fleshy appendage on the muzzle), consisting of an anterior horseshoe-shaped leaf, various accessory leaves, and an upright transverse leaf. They are found in the tropics from Africa through Asia to Australia. Hipposiderine bats range in colour from reddish or grayish through brown to almost black. Head and body length is about 3–11 cm (1.2–4.3 inches); the tail is either entirely lacking or, when present, measures up to 6 cm (2.4 inches) long. Most hipposiderine species are gregarious and shelter in caves or similar roosts, although a few are solitary.

A coastal cave filled with roundleaf bats on the island of Bioko, northwest of Equatorial Guinea, western Africa. Joel Sartore/National Geographic Image Collection/Getty Images

THERMOREGULATION

When fully active, bats have a body temperature of about 37 °C (98.6 °F). Although some bats maintain fairly even body temperatures, a large number undergo periodic raising or lowering of their temperature. Many of the vesper bats and horseshoe bats and a few free-tailed bats reduce their body temperature to that of their surroundings (ambient temperature) shortly after coming to rest. This condition is called heterothermy. They raise their temperature again on being aroused or when readying themselves for nocturnal foraging. The drop in body temperature, if the ambient temperature is relatively low, results in a lethargic state. Energy is conserved by thus "turning down the thermostat," but the bat is rendered relatively unresponsive to threats by predators or weather. Heterothermic bats therefore generally roost in secluded sites offering protection, often in crevices. In heterothermic bats one or more sensory systems and the brain remain sensitive at low temperatures and initiate the necessary heat production for arousal. Heat is generated by the metabolism of fat and by shivering.

Many bats that exhibit daily torpor also hibernate during the winter and therefore must store energy as body fat. In the fall these bats increase their weight by 50 to 100 percent. They must also migrate from the summer roost to a suitable hibernation site (often a cave) that will remain cool and humid throughout the winter without freezing. Large populations often aggregate in such caves. Hibernation involves the absence of temperature regulation for long periods in addition to adaptations of circulation, respiration, and renal (kidney) function and the suspension of most aspects of activity. Bats of hibernating species generally court and mate in the fall when they are at their nutritional peak. During pregnancy, lactation, and juvenile growth, bats probably thermoregulate differently, more closely approximating stability.

Bats of several tropical families maintain a constant body temperature (homeothermy). This, however, depends on the nutritional state as well. A spectrum of degrees of homeothermy and heterothermy probably will be discovered.

PHYLLOSTOMIDAE

Phyllostomidae is a family of approximately 150 species of tropical and subtropical bats known collectively as American leaf-nosed bats. Phyllostomid bats are native to the New World from the United States to Argentina and are found in habitats ranging from forests to deserts. Their features vary, but most species are broad-winged and have a simple, spear-shaped structure—the nose leaf—on the muzzle. Coloration of the fur ranges within and among the species from gray, pale brown, and dark brown to orange, red, yellow, or whitish; some species, such as the tent-making bat (*Uroderma bilobatum*), have striped faces. Phyllostomatid bats are 4.0–13.5 cm (1.6–5.3 inches) without the tail, which may be absent or up to 5.5 cm (2.2 inches) long. The largest member of the family is the spectral bat (*Vampyrum spectrum*); it is 12.5–13.5 cm (4.9–5.3 inches) long with a wingspan of 90 cm (35 inches) or more.

The diet of phyllostomid bats varies. Some, such as the little big-eared bats (*Micronycteris*), are insect eaters; some larger forms are carnivorous. Many other species feed on fruit, nectar, or pollen; among these are the nectar-feeding bats in the Tribe Glossophaginae, which are equipped with specialized long snouts and tongues for feeding. This family also includes the vampire bats (subfamily Desmodontinae).

Phyllostomid bats usually live in small groups; some, such as the short-tailed bats (*Carollia*), form colonies of several hundred. Roosting sites include caves, tree hollows, buildings, and the undersides of bridges. The tent-making bats and the several other fruit-eating bats (e.g., *Artibeus*) modify leaves to create shelters; they roost on the undersides of palm and other plant leaves after biting across the leaves to make the ends hang downward.

DIGESTION AND WATER CONSERVATION

Digestion in bats is unusually rapid. They chew and fragment their food exceptionally thoroughly and thus expose a large surface area of it to digestive action. They may begin to defecate 30 to 60 minutes after beginning to feed and thereby reduce the load that must be carried in flight.

Some bats live in sun-baked roosts without access to water during the day. They may choose these roosts for their heat, and thus conserve their own, but it is not yet known how they hold their body temperature down without using water. In the laboratory, bats die if body temperature rises above about 40–41 °C (104–106 °F).

SENSES

In folklore, bats have been considered to be blind. In fact, the eyes in the Microchiroptera are small and have not been well studied. Among the Megachiroptera the eyes are large, but vision has been studied in detail only in flying foxes. These bats are able to make visual discriminations at lower light levels than humans can. The Megachiroptera fly at night, of course, and some genera fly below or in the jungle canopy, where light levels are very low. Except for rousette bats (*Rousettus*), none are known to orient acoustically.

Studies of several genera of Microchiroptera have revealed that vision is used in long-distance navigation and that obstacles and motion can be detected visually. Bats also presumably use vision to distinguish day from night and to synchronize their internal clocks with the local cycle of daylight and darkness.

The senses of taste, smell, and touch in bats do not seem to be strikingly different from those of related mammals. Smell is probably used as an aid in locating fruit and flowers and possibly, in the case of vampire bats, large vertebrates. It may also be used for locating an occupied roost, members of the same species, and the differentiation of individuals by sex. Many bats depend upon touch, aided by well-developed facial and toe whiskers and possibly by the projecting tail, to place themselves in comforting body contact with rock surfaces or with other bats in the roost.

EVOLUTION AND PALEONTOLOGY

The fossil record of bats prior to the Pleistocene Epoch (about 2,600,000 to 11,700 years ago) is limited and reveals little about bat evolution. Most fossils can be attributed to living families. Skulls and teeth compatible with early bats are known from about 60 million years ago, during the Paleocene Epoch. These specimens, however, may well have been from insectivores, from which bats are clearly distinguishable only on the basis of flight adaptations. By 45 million years ago (the Eocene Epoch), bats with fully developed powers of flight had evolved.

The order Chiroptera is readily divided into two suborders—Megachiroptera (large Old World fruit bats) and Microchiroptera (small bats). The Megachiroptera orient visually and exhibit a number of primitive skeletal features. The Microchiroptera orient acoustically. It is not certain that they have a common origin. The suborders either evolved separately from flightless insectivores or diverged very early in chiropteran history.

The two principal geographic centres of bat evolution appear to be the Australo-Malaysian region, with about 290 species, and the New World tropics, with about 230 species. Comparable ecological niches in the Old World and the New World are occupied largely by different genera of bats, usually of different families.

TYPES OF BATS

The various bat groups may be classified geographically as well as taxonomically. It is often useful to separate bats into Old World and New World groups and groups that are distributed globally.

OLD WORLD BATS

Hundreds of species are native to Africa, Eurasia, Australia, and Oceania. Old World groups include the horseshoe bats and Old World fruit bats, as well as the flying foxes, a diverse and widespread group that ranges from Africa and Eurasia to Indonesia and Australia.

BARBASTELLES

Either of two bats of the vesper bat family, Vespertilionidae, the barbastelles (genus *Barbastella*) are found in Europe and North Africa (*B. barbastellus*) and in the Middle East and Asia (*B. leucomelas*). Barbastelles have short, wide ears that are joined on the forehead. Their fur is long and dark, with hairs tipped in white or gray. A barbastelle's body is about 4–6 cm (1.6–2.4 inches) long; the tail is about the same length. Weight is about 6–10 grams (0.2–0.3 ounce). Relatively heavy fliers, barbastelles live alone or in small groups and roost in trees or buildings. From fall to spring they hibernate in caves.

FLYING FOXES

Flying foxes (genus *Pteropus*), which are also called fox bats, constitute any of about 65 bat species found on tropical islands from Madagascar to Australia and Indonesia and mainland Asia. They are the largest bats; some attain a wingspan of 1.5 m (5 feet), with a head and body length of about 40 cm (16 inches).

Flying foxes are Old World fruit bats (family Pteropodidae) that roost in large numbers and eat fruit. They are therefore a potential pest and cannot be imported into the United States. Like nearly all Old World fruit bats, flying foxes use sight rather than echolocation to navigate.

Flying fox bat (Pteropus) *on the island of Bali, Indonesia.* Shutterstock.com

HORSESHOE BATS

There are almost 80 species of horseshoe bats (genus *Rhinolophus*), a group of large-eared, insect-eating bats that make up the sole genus of family Rhinolophidae. Their taxonomic name refers to the large, complex nose leaf consisting of a fleshy structure on the muzzle. Of the three "leaf" sections, one resembles a horseshoe, hence their common name. The exact function of these facial appurtenances has yet to be determined, but scientists believe they may help to direct outgoing echolocation calls.

Horseshoe bats are found in tropical and temperate regions from Europe to Japan and from Asia to Africa. They are usually brown but occasionally are red. They are about 3.5–11 cm (1.4–4.3 inches) long without the 2.5–4.5-cm (1–1.8-inch) tail, and they weigh 5–30 grams (0.17–1 ounce). Horseshoe bats live in groups and roost in damp, dark places such as caves. Species native to temperate regions hibernate in winter.

NEW ZEALAND SHORT-TAILED BATS

There are two species of New Zealand short-tailed bats (*Mystacina robusta* and *M. tuberculata*). These small bats are the only species in the rare bat family Mystacinidae, which is found only in New Zealand. They are about 6–7 cm (2.4–2.8 inches) long and have a short 1.8-cm (0.7-inch) tail. The fur is grayish brown and thicker than the fur of other bats. Close to the body the wing membranes are leathery, and the wings can be furled tightly within them. *M. tuberculata* is the most terrestrial bat, and it is very agile on the ground. In its forest habitat it may roost in hollow trees, caves, or crevices, and it sometimes digs tunnels in rotten wood. The diet of this species includes fruit, nectar, pollen, and insects. The young are born with their eyes open. *M. robusta* is probably extinct.

NOCTULES

The world's six extant species of noctules (genus *Nyctalus*) are found in Europe and Asia. They are vesper bats (family Vespertilionidae). Noctule coloration ranges from golden to yellowish or dark brown, with a paler underside. They are 5–10 cm (2–4 inches) long without the 3.5–6.5-cm (1.4–2.6-inch) tail. Noctules are swift, erratic fliers and commonly leave their roosts (generally in caves or buildings) at or before sunset. They eat insects and apparently are fond of beetles. The best-known and most widely distributed species is the Eurasian *N. noctula*, a reddish brown migratory inhabitant of wooded regions.

OLD WORLD FRUIT BATS

Old World fruit bats (family Pteropodidae) constitute a group of more than 180 species of large-eyed fruit-eating or flower-feeding bats widely distributed from Africa to Southeast Asia and Australia. Some species are solitary, some gregarious. Most roost in the open in trees, but some inhabit caves, rocks, or buildings.

Among the best-known pteropodids are the flying foxes (*Pteropus*), found on tropical islands from Madagascar to Australia and Indonesia. They are the largest of all bats. Some of the smallest members of the family are the pollen- and

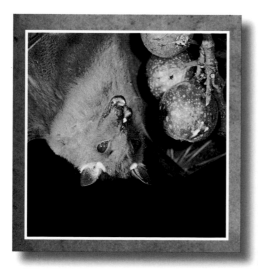

Epauletted fruit bat (Epomophorus wahlbergi) *feeding on wild figs.* Jane Burton/ Bruce Coleman Inc.

nectar-eating long-tongued fruit bats (*Macroglossus*), which attain a head and body length of about 6–7 cm (2.4–2.8 inches) and a wingspan of about 25 cm (10 inches). Colour varies among the pteropodids; some are red or yellow, some striped or spotted. With the exception of rousette bats (*Rousettus*), Old World fruit bats rely on vision rather than echolocation (animal "sonar") as a means of avoiding obstacles.

Asian representatives of the family include various tube-nosed bats and the abundant short-nosed fruit bats (*Cynopterus*). Among African members of the family are the epauletted fruit bats (*Epomophorus*), in which the male has tufts of pale hair on the shoulders, and the hammer-headed fruit bat (*Hypsignathus monstrosus*), which has a large, blunt muzzle and pendulous lips.

SLIT-FACED BATS

All 16 species of slit-faced bats (which are also called hollow-faced bats) belong to the genus *Nycteris*, which constitutes the family Nycteridae. Slit-faced bats inhabit tropical areas in Africa. They are also found in the Malaysian and Indonesian regions.

Slit-faced bats have a longitudinal hollow on their faces and a nose leaf (fleshy structure on the muzzle) that is split in the centre. They are about 5–8 cm (2–3 inches) long, excluding a tail of about the same length, weigh 10–30 grams (0.3–1 ounce), and are usually grayish to brown. The tail has T-shaped cartilage on the end, which helps to support the membrane that connects the thighs. They eat insects and usually roost in dark, humid shelters, such as caves, tree hollows, small buildings, and animal burrows.

NEW WORLD BATS

Although many bat species inhabit North America, many New World families are concentrated in the warmer areas of Central and South America. Bulldog bats, disk-winged bats, fringe-lipped bats, and others, including all of the world's vampire bats, are native to Central and South America. Notable North American species include the hoary bat and the red bat.

BULLDOG BATS

Bulldog bats (family Noctilionidae) reside in tropical areas of Central and South America. They are among the few bats known that routinely forage low over water. Both species have full lips and a flat, squarish muzzle very similar to that of a bulldog. Bulldog bats have long, narrow wings and long, pointed ears, their most distinctive feature being their large hind feet. Wide and flat with long, hooklike claws, they are well adapted to snatching prey from the surface of still water.

The lesser bulldog bat (*Noctilio albiventris,* formerly *N. labialis*) is about 9 cm (3.5 inches) long with a wingspan of 40–44 cm (15.7–17.3 inches). The greater bulldog, or fisherman, bat (*N. leporinus*) is considerably larger, with a length of 11–12 cm (4.3–4.7 inches) and a wingspan of up to 70 cm (27.5 inches). Greater bulldog bats weigh about twice that of the lesser. The short fur of both ranges in colour from brown to reddish or orange; the scientific name of the lesser bulldog bat, *N. albiventris*, indicates its whitish belly. An oily substance that acts as a water repellent covers the wings and large tail membrane of both species; both also swim well. Bulldog bats are widespread in tropical lowlands, where they roost in colonies during the day. The greater bulldog bat specializes in catching fish for food; the lesser feeds mostly on insects.

Greater and lesser bulldog bats employ a variety of hunting strategies. They use sound to detect small ripples in the water created by fish or fluttering insects on the surface. The bat then uses its hind feet to seize and carry off the victim. Occasionally, when prey density is high or when the bats return to areas where they have hunted successfully before, they will drag their claws through the water for several metres, catching prey at random without using echolocation. Insects are also taken in mid-air with a wing or the tail membrane. After capture, the prey is transferred to the mouth, briefly chewed, then stored in the large cheek pouches characteristic of these bats.

The two *Noctilio* species constitute the entire family Noctilionidae, although the name *bulldog bat* is sometimes also given to the bats of the family Molossidae.

Disk-Winged Bats

Disk-winged bats (family Thyropteridae) make up three species of bats inhabiting Central America and northern South America. They are distinguished by round disks at the base of the thumb and on the sole of the foot. The disks act as suction cups and enable the bats to cling to smooth surfaces. One disk alone is capable of supporting the weight of the bat's body. Disk-winged bats are small, reddish-brown bats, about 3.4 to 5.2 cm (1.4 to 2 inches) in length with tails about 2.5 to 3.3 cm (0.9 to 1.3 inches) long. Average weight is approximately 4 grams (0.14 ounce). Spix's disk-winged bat (*Thyroptera tricolor*) lives in small, cohesive colonies that roost in rolled-up leaves. It is unique among bats for its "heads-up" roosting posture.

Fringe-Lipped Bats

Fringe-lipped bats (*Trachops cirrhosus*), which are also called frog-eating bats, are characterized by the fleshy tubercles that cover their chin. The fringe-lipped bat is widespread in tropical lowland forests of Central and South America. It has large feet with robust claws, a well-developed membrane between its legs, and large ears. Considered medium-sized, it attains a maximum length of about 10 cm (4 inches) and a maximum weight of 45 grams (1.6 ounces). The brownish fur is woolly and rather coarse. The bat's call is similar to that of the nonpredatory Jamaican fruit bat (*Artibeus jamaicensis*). The fringe-lipped bat can discriminate poisonous from nonpoisonous frogs by their species-specific calls. It is also presumed that the fleshy tubercles on the bat's chin allow perception of chemicals in the frog's skin.

Although the fringe-lipped bat is best known for its frog-eating habits, its diet frequently includes large quantities of insects and small vertebrates such as lizards. To find food, fringe-lipped bats fly continuously up and down ravines or in circles over ponds, listening for the mating calls of male frogs and katydids. After detecting potential prey, the bat approaches, covering the site with its wings and tail membrane. Using its head to search for the prey under its wings, the bat immobilizes the prey with a bite and, holding the victim in its mouth, flies to a feeding perch.

The fringe-lipped bat is classified as a leaf-nosed bat (family Phyllostomatidae), a very large family that also includes the fishing bat.

Hoary Bats

Hoary bats (*Lasiurus cinereus*) are migratory North American bats found in wooded areas from Canada to Mexico. The species is one of the vesper bats, family Vespertilionidae, and measures 13–14 cm (5–5.5 inches) long, including a 5- to 6-cm (2- to 2.5-inch) tail; weight is about 30 grams (1 ounce). Its thick fur is yellowish or reddish brown and is tipped, or frosted, with silver. A strong-flying, solitary insect eater, the hoary bat roosts in trees, where the colour of its fur blends with that of lichen-covered bark. A subspecies of *L. cinereus* is the only bat in the Hawaiian Islands.

JAMAICAN FRUIT BATS

Jamaican fruit bats (*Artibeus jamaicensis*), which are also called Mexican fruit bats, are common and widespread across Central and South America. They are distinguished by a fleshy nose leaf resembling a third ear positioned on the muzzle. The Jamaican fruit bat has gray-brown fur and indistinct, whitish facial stripes. It has no tail, and the membrane stretching between its legs is small and u-shaped. Its length is about 9 cm (3.5 inches). Although compared to other New World fruit bats, the Jamaican fruit bat is one of the heavier species, weighing 40–65 grams (1.4–2.3 ounces). This bat smells like perfumed soap.

Some Jamaican fruit bats fly up to 10–15 km (6–9 miles) per night between their day roost and their feeding sites. To orient in the dark, they emit sweeping, high-frequency calls and analyze the echoes reflecting off of obstacles. The Jamaican fruit bat feeds on a variety of fruits, including both native and cultivated plants such as wild figs, cecropia, guava, papaya, and banana. Depending on the seasonal availability of food, its diet may also contain nectar, pollen, leaves, and, rarely, a few insects. They have reportedly damaged crops of cultivated fruit.

To find fruit-bearing trees, the Jamaican fruit bat hones in on the specific scent of ripe fruit. At night, dozens and sometimes hundreds of bats may visit a single tree. The bats first circle the tree, then approach a selected fruit and take it in flight or in a brief landing. The fruit is then transported by mouth to a nearby, temporary dining roost. The bat takes a bite, chews the pulp thoroughly, presses it with its tongue against its rigid palate, and swallows the juice. The remaining dry pellet is dropped. Seeds of large-seeded fruits are discarded at the feeding roost, whereas small seeds are swallowed and excreted (whole) in flight. Owing to its frugivorous (fruit-eating) feeding habits and rapid digestion (a mere 15–20 minutes from ingestion to excretion), this bat plays an important role in seed dispersal and the regeneration of New World tropical forests.

The Jamaican fruit bat preferably roosts in hollow trees, caves, or foliage, with the males forming harems and defending roost sites. Other males may hang in nearby foliage. Females are able to reproduce immediately after giving birth (postpartum estrus), and after fertilization the gestation period is largely linked to the seasonal availability of fruit. Gestation can vary from as little as four weeks up to several months. Births are single but are synchronized within a population, resulting in one to two birth peaks annually. Their life expectancy in the wild rarely exceeds two or three years. Although opossums prey upon them, the bats emit distress calls when captured, thus summoning a hoard of others to its defense.

The Jamaican fruit bat is one of about 14 *Artibeus* species, all of which are large, New World fruit bats. Up to four *Artibeus* species may coexist in a given locale. The genus *Artibeus* belongs to the New World family of leaf-nosed bats.

Red Bats

Red bats (*Lasiurus borealis*), which are also called Eastern red bats, are a migratory vesper bat (family Vespertilionidae) found in wooded areas of North America. The red bat is about 10 cm (4 inches) long, including a 5-cm (2-inch) tail, weighs 10–15 grams (0.33–0.5 ounce), and has narrow wings and short, rounded ears. The fur is fairly long, chestnut to rusty in colour, and tipped with white. The red bat is a strong, swift flier that spirals down from heights to feed primarily on moths. It also takes flies and beetles and even hunts crickets and cicadas on the ground. Unlike most other bats, it is solitary and bears as many as four young in a single litter.

SMOKY BATS

Smoky bats are found in the Central and South American tropics. The two known species constitute family Furipteridae. *Amorphochilus schnablii* is the smoky bat, whereas *Furipterus horrens* is also commonly called the thumbless bat. Small and delicately built, both species range in size from about 3.7 to 5.8 cm (1.5 to 2.3 inches), have tails about 2.4 to 3.6 cm (1 to 1.4 inches) in length, and weigh about 3 to 5 grams (0.1 to 0.16 ounce). These slate-gray or brown bats are notable for their reduced thumbs, which are covered by the wing membranes up to the base of their functionless claws. Both species are rarely seen, and very little is known about their habits.

VAMPIRE BATS

The three known species of vampire bats (family Desmodontidae) are native to the New World tropics and subtropics. The common vampire bat (*Desmodus rotundus*), together with the white-winged vampire bat (*Diaemus*, or *Desmodus, youngi*) and the hairy-legged vampire bat (*Diphylla ecaudata*) are the only sanguivorous (blood-eating) bats. The common vampire bat thrives in agricultural areas and feeds on livestock such as cattle, pigs, and chickens. The other two vampires are primarily restricted to intact forests, where they feed on birds, reptiles, and other forest animals.

Common vampire bats are tailless and are considered medium-sized, with a length of 7–9 cm (2.8–3.5 inches). Weight is variable owing to the large volume of blood that the bat ingests. A 57-gram (2-ounce) specimen, for example, can double its weight in one feeding. Its fur is short, ranging in colour from brown to reddish orange; its wings are long and pointed; and the first segments of the thumb are exceptionally long, enabling it to hop and creep in a strangely agile, yet froglike manner along the ground. The common vampire bat is the only bat capable of taking off from the ground, using its long thumbs to leap a metre (three feet) or more into the air before flying off.

At night, the bats emerge from their roosts in hollow trees or caves. Using sonar for orientation, they detect the presence of prey with heat sensors located in the face. The bats will usually land near their resting prey and then hop or crawl toward it. Once they have reached their prey (which can include sleeping humans), they make a tiny incision in the skin with their razor-sharp incisor teeth. The incision usually goes unnoticed by the resting animals, and the bats subsequently lick the blood flowing from the tiny wound. A very strong anticoagulant in the saliva of vampire bats keeps the

Vampire bat (Desmodus rotundus), *Costa Rica. Vampire bats bite an animal's skin until the blood flows freely and then lick the blood with their tongue.* Michael & Patricia Fogden/Minden Pictures/Getty Images

blood from clotting. Although the wounds themselves are usually not serious, infection may result. Vampire bats are considered pests in much of their range, as they frequently transmit rabies to livestock. Humans can also be infected.

The common vampire bat is noted for its unusual and highly evolved social structure. When an individual bat in a group does not get enough food at night, members of its group share their blood meals. Births are single but, unlike other bats that are usually weaned after four to six weeks, young vampires stay with their mothers for several months until they have learned to feed on their own. Females and their young form stable groups that roost together. Males roost separately, except for dominant males who roost with the females.

Vampire bats are related to the New World leaf-nosed bats and are sometimes classified with them as a subfamily (Desmodontinae). The New World false vampire bats (genera *Vampyrum* and *Chrotopterus*) are phyllostomatids that are much larger than the sanguivorous bats. Although *Vampyrum* species are fierce in appearance, their snouts and long canine teeth are used to capture and eat small prey. Various Old World false vampire bats are found in Africa, Asia, and Australia.

GLOBALLY DISTRIBUTED FORMS

Other groups of bats are found worldwide. The brown bats and vesper bats occur on every continent except Antarctica. All free-tailed and many leaf-nosed bats prefer the warmer parts of the world. Although most ghost bats reside in the New World tropics, one species lives in Australia. False vampire bats are known in both the Old World and New World.

Brown Bats

Brown bats belong to the genera *Myotis* (little brown bats) and *Eptesicus* (big brown bats). Both are vesper bats, widely distributed (being found in almost all parts of the world), and insectivorous.

The genus *Myotis* includes more than 80 species, among them the little brown bat (*M. lucifugus*) of North America and the large mouse-eared bat (*M. myotis*) of Europe. Members of the genus are about 3.5–8 cm (about 1.4–3.1 inches) long without the 4- to 6-cm (1.6- to 2.4-inch) tail and weigh about 5–45 grams (0.2–1.6 ounces). Apart from humans, they are probably the most widespread genus of land mammals.

Included in the genus *Eptesicus* are more than 30 species commonly referred to as big brown bats or serotines. These bats are 3.5 to 7.5 cm long without the 3.5- to 5.5-cm tail. They are relatively slow, heavy fliers and are often found in buildings and hollow trees. The big brown bat (*E. fuscus*) is a common North American species, and the serotine (*E. serotinus*) is a stoutly built Eurasian form.

False Vampire Bats

False vampire bats belong to the Old World genera *Megaderma, Cardioderma,* and *Macroderma* (family Megadermatidae) and the New World genera *Vampyrum* and *Chrotopterus* (family Phyllostomatidae). They are conspicuous because of their large size and originally thought to feed on blood, as do the true vampire bats. The false vampires are now known to be carnivorous, preying mainly on small vertebrates such as other bats, lizards, and mice.

These large, grayish or brownish bats range in size from 6.5 cm (about 2.5 inches) for *Megaderma* species up to 14 cm (5.5 inches) for the Australian false vampire, or ghost, bat (*Macroderma gigas*), the largest bat in the suborder Microchiroptera. The tropical American false vampire (*Vampyrum spectrum*), measuring about 13.5 cm (5.3 inches), is the largest New World bat. False vampires are tailless (except *Chrotopterus,* which has a tiny tail), and each species has a conspicuous nose leaf (a flap of skin and connective tissue around the nostrils) and large rounded ears. In the megadermatids the ears are joined at the base, which may help stabilize them during flight, and the eyes are relatively large.

False vampires roost in caves and hollow trees; *Vampyrum* species often roost in pairs with some of their offspring. The African false vampire (*Cardioderma cor*), which eats mostly large invertebrates, forages by hanging in wait, listening for its prey. The capture is made with a short, rapid flight. The Australian false vampire is considered an endangered species.

FREE-TAILED BATS

About 100 species of free-tailed bats, which are also called mastiff bats and belong to the family Molossidae, are known to exist. Free-tailed bats are so named for the way in which part of the tail extends somewhat beyond the membrane connecting the hind legs. Some free-tailed bats are also known as mastiff bats because their faces bear a superficial resemblance to those dogs.

Swift fliers with long, slender wings, free-tailed bats are small-eyed, often heavy-snouted bats about 4 to 13 cm (1.6 to 5.1 inches) long excluding the 1.5- to 8-cm (0.6- to 3.1-inch) tail. Their ears are large and are joined across the forehead in some species. Except for the naked, or hairless, bat (*Cheiromeles torquatus*), which is almost hairless, they have short, velvety, usually dark fur.

Free-tailed bats eat insects and roost in tree hollows, caves, and buildings. They are found worldwide in warm regions. Most species live in groups, and some form colonies with populations numbering in the millions, such as the Mexican free-tailed bat (*Tadarida brasiliensis mexicana*) colonies at Carlsbad Caverns National Park and in downtown Austin, Texas. In the past, guano was mined from caves in which the bats roosted, used both as fertilizer and to produce sodium nitrate for gunpowder. Free-tailed bats do not hibernate, but some species migrate seasonally.

GHOST BATS

Ghost bats are some of the few bats known to possess white or gray fur. However, not every bat with white fur is called a ghost bat. Ghost bats are tropical, but only one, also called the Australian giant false vampire bat (*Macroderma gigas*), is found outside Central and South America. The four ghost bat species of the New World belong to the genus *Diclidurus*.

D. albus is snowy-white with dark eyes, yellow-edged ears, and long, nearly transparent wings. Males bear a peculiar hook-shaped ornament on their tail membrane, the function of which is unclear. Compared to other insect-eating bats, *D. albus* is medium-sized, with a length of about 9 cm (3.5 inches), a body mass of about 20 grams (0.7 ounce), and a wingspan of about 40 cm (16 inches). This species is widely distributed in tropical lowland forest and open areas throughout Central and South America. Its diet consists mostly of moths, which are captured in midair with the large tail membrane and often with the help of a wing. While in flight, this bat continuously emits high-pitched, nearly constant-frequency signals, most of which are inaudible to humans. The echoes of their calls transmit information about type, position, flight speed, and direction of their insect prey. The signals emitted by these bats are well suited to the open habitats in which they hunt and are very different from the calls of fruit bats, which fly within the forest canopy. Although ghost bats were once considered rare, recent studies using electronic listening equipment indicate that they can be rather common locally. Their abundance suggests that they can play important roles in controlling insect populations.

    D. albus and the other *Diclidurus* species belong to the family Emballonuridae, whereas another New World ghost bat, also known as the Honduran white bat (*Ectophylla alba*), is a leaf-nosed bat. The Australian ghost bat is a larger, grayish bat of the family Megadermatidae.

Leaf-Nosed Bats

Almost 250 species of New World and Old World bats belonging to the families Phyllostomidae and Hipposideridae are called leaf-nosed bats. Each species possesses a flat projection on the muzzle that often resembles a leaf. As is the case with Old World horseshoe

Short-tailed leaf-nosed bat. The leaf-like projection on the nose is believed to help with echolocation. Thomas Lohnes/AFP/Getty Images

bats, the purpose of the leaf structure is not known for certain, but it may aid in echolocation.

Family Phyllostomidae is known collectively as American leaf-nosed bats. Phyllostomid bats classified into 55 genera and 160 species. They are found from the United States to Argentina in habitats ranging from forest to desert. Their features vary, but most are broad-winged and have a simple spearhead-shaped structure on the muzzle that is called the nose leaf. Coloration of the fur ranges from gray, pale brown, and dark brown to orange, red, yellow, or whitish; some species, such as the tent-making bat (*Uroderma bilobatum*), have striped faces. American leaf-nosed bats are 4–13.5 cm (1.6–5.3 inches) without the tail, which may be absent or up to 5.5 cm (2.2 inches) long. The largest member of the family is the spectral bat (*Vampyrum spectrum*), sometimes called a false vampire bat; it can have a wingspan of 90 cm (35 inches) or more.

The diet of phyllostomid bats varies. Some, such as the little big-eared bats (*Micronycteris*), are insect eaters; some larger forms are carnivorous. Others feed on fruit, nectar, or pollen; nectar-feeding bats are equipped with specialized long snouts and tongues for feeding. This family also includes the vampire bats.

Phyllostomid bats usually live in small groups; some, such as the short-tailed bats (*Carollia*), form colonies of several hundred. Roosting sites include caves, tree hollows, buildings, and the undersides of bridges. The tent-making bats and several fruit-eating bats (e.g., *Artibeus*) modify leaves to create shelters. They roost on the undersides of palm and other plant leaves after biting across the leaves to make the ends hang downward.

Family Hipposideridae, known as the Old World leaf-nosed bats, is characterized by a round nose leaf consisting of a horseshoe-shaped forward leaf, various accessory leaves, and an upright leaf. These bats are found in the tropics from

Africa and across Asia to Australia. They range in colour from reddish or grayish through brown to almost black. Head and body length is about 3–11 cm (1.2–4.3 inches); the tail either is entirely lacking or, when present, measures up to 6 cm (about 2.4 inches) long. Old World leaf-nosed bats are classified into 9 genera; most of the 81 species shelter in caves or similar roosts, although a few are solitary.

Long-Eared Bats

Long-eared bats, which are also called lump-nosed bats or big-eared bats, are small, usually colony-dwelling vesper bats (family Vespertilionidae). The 19 extant species are found in both the Old World and the New World (*Plecotus*) and in Australia (*Nyctophilus*). They are approximately 4–7 cm (1.6–2.8 inches) long, not including the 3.5- to 5.5-cm

The ears of a gray long-eared bat (Plecotus austriacus) *are three quarters the length of the head and body.* Shutterstock.com

(1.4–2.2-inch) tail, and weigh 5–20 grams (0.2–0.7 ounce). They have soft brown fur, and some species have glandular lumps on the muzzle. The ears, which may be 4 cm (1.6 inches) long, are folded when the bats rest. Long-eared bats fly slowly and frequently hover to pick insects from leaves or walls. Like many bats found in temperate regions, they hibernate in winter instead of migrating.

Pipistrelles

The 68 species of pipistrelles (genus *Pipistrellus*) belong to the vesper bat family (Vespertilionidae). Pipistrelles are found in almost all parts of the world. They are grayish, brown, reddish, or black bats that are about 3.5–10 cm (1.4–4 inches) long, not including the tail, which may be 2.5–6 cm (1–2.4 inches) long.

Erratic fliers, they appear before most other bats in the evening and sometimes even fly about during the day. Representatives include *P. pipistrellus* of Eurasia and the eastern (*P. subflavus*) and western (*P. hesperus*) pipistrelles of North America.

Sheath-Tailed Bats

The approximately 50 species of sheath-tailed bats (family Emballonuridae), which are also called sac-winged bats, are named for the way in which the tail protrudes from a sheath in the membrane attached to the hind legs. The term *sac-winged* refers to the glandular sacs in the wing membranes of several genera.

Sheath-tailed bats are found worldwide in tropical and subtropical regions. They are usually black, brown, or gray, and some are striped or mottled. They are about 4–10 cm (1.6–4 inches) long, without the 0.6- to 3-cm (0.2- to 1.2-inch) tail, and they weigh about 5–30 grams (0.2–1 ounce). Compared with other bats, they shelter in relatively open places, such as shallow caves.

Among the 13 genera of the family are the sac-winged bats (*Saccopteryx*), which are white-striped bats of Central and South America; ghost bats (*Diclidurus*), which are white or white and gray bats of the New World; and tomb bats (*Taphozous*), which are swift-flying bats found from Africa through southern Asia to Australia.

VESPER BATS

Vesper bats (family Vespertilionidae), which are also called evening bats, number more than 400 species. They are found worldwide in both tropical and temperate regions, their habitats ranging from tropical forest to desert.

Vesper bats have small eyes and well-developed tails. Most species have long wings, and some have very large ears. The fur is generally gray, brown, or blackish, but it may be red, as in the red bat (*Lasiurus borealis*), grizzled, as in particoloured bats (*Vespertilio*), or marked with white, as in spotted bats (*Euderma*). The lesser bamboo bat, one of the smallest of bats, is about 4 cm (1.5 inches) in head and body length; it weighs about 2 grams (0.07 ounce) and has a wingspan of 15 cm (6 inches). Other species range up to 10 cm (4 inches) in head and body length and 50 grams (1.8 ounces) in weight.

Most vesper bats feed on insects, often catching their prey in the membrane between their hind legs before seizing the insect with their teeth. A few species of mouse-eared, or little brown, bats (*Myotis*) prey on fish. In general, vesper bats live in colonies and roost in caves, hollow trees, and similar shelters. Some have been found in the twigs of birds' nests and in roof thatching; others habitually roost in branches, on tree trunks, or in the hollow core of bamboo stalks. Many that inhabit temperate regions hibernate or migrate in winter.

Other vesper bats include pipistrelles, noctules, hoary bats, barbastelles, and long-eared bats.

CHAPTER 7
XENARTHRANS

Xenarthrans (magnorder Xenarthra) belong to an ancient lineage of mammals comprising the armadillos (order Cingulata) and the sloths and anteaters (order Pilosa). The namesake feature shared by all members of Xenarthra is seen in the lower backbone. The lumbar vertebrae are "xenarthrous"; that is, they have extra contacts (joints, or arthroses) that function to strengthen the lower back and hips. This aids use of the forelegs in activities not associated with locomotion, such as digging—the primary method used by anteaters and armadillos to obtain food.

Xenarthran diets range from strictly insectivorous in anteaters, which eat only ants and termites, to strictly folivorous in sloths, which eat only leaves. Armadillos, not nearly as specialized, eat a variety of plant matter and small animals. Xenarthran metabolisms, however, are similar in that all are low compared with those of other mammals; some burn calories at less than half the rate expected for mammals of similar size. As a result, xenarthrans eat less than other mammals and have body temperatures that are a few degrees cooler.

Present distribution of xenarthrans is restricted to Latin America, the exception being the nine-banded armadillo (*Dasypus novemcinctus*), whose range extends into the southern United States. Additionally, the pangolin (page 216), while historically grouped with these mammals, is actually anatomically distinct and is found in both Asia and Africa.

ORDER CINGULATA

Order Cingulata consists primarily of armoured armadillo-like animals, and the name refers to the girdlelike

Glyptodont (genus Glyptodon*).* Courtesy of the trustees of the British Museum (Natural History); photograph, Imitor

shell of present-day armadillos. The armadillo family (Dasypodidae), with 8 genera and 20 species, is the only surviving family of Cingulata. Five other families in this order are extinct and are known only from fossil remains. Members of extinct families include glyptodonts and huge North American armadillos.

ORDER PILOSA

Sloths and anteaters are the living members of the order Pilosa, whose name refers to the animals' hairiness. Three families exist today, encompassing five genera and nine species. Six families, primarily ground sloths, are extinct. The order Pilosa is further subdivided into the suborder Vermilingua (literally "worm-tongue" in Latin), which is descriptive of the long slender tongue of anteaters, and the suborder Phyllophaga, meaning "leaf-eater," descriptive of the diet of sloths.

PALEONTOLOGY

Xenarthrans are known only from the Western Hemisphere and arose in South America during the Paleocene Epoch (65.5 million to 55.8 million years ago). The fossil record shows that the group was both more diverse and more widely distributed as recently as the Pleistocene Epoch (2,600,000 to 11,700 years ago), when ground sloths colonized the islands of the Greater Antilles and glyptodonts, ground sloths such as *Megatherium*, and giant armadillos roamed North America. At least one species of ground sloth reached present-day Alaska.

ARMADILLOS, SLOTHS, AND ANTEATERS

Modern xenarthrans are represented by 29 species of armadillos, sloths, and anteaters. By far, the armadillos are the most diverse and widespread. Sloths, on the other hand, reside in the warm lowland forests of the New World tropics. Both anteaters and armadillos can be found in the forests and savanna habitats of Latin America.

ARMADILLOS

Armadillos (family Dasypodidae) are armoured mammals found mainly in tropical and subtropical regions of Central and South America. Most of the 20 species inhabit open areas, such as grasslands, but some also live in forests. All armadillos possess a set of plates called the carapace that covers much of the body, including the head and, in most species, the legs and tail. In all but one species the carapace is nearly hairless. The carapace is made of bony transverse bands covered with tough scales that are derived from skin tissue. The three-, six-, and nine-banded armadillos are named for the number of movable bands in their armour. Only one species, the nine-banded armadillo, *Dasypus novemcinctus*, is found in the United States. Its range has expanded into several southern states since it was first observed in Texas during the 1800s. Eight-banded individuals of this species are common in some regions.

Southernmost armadillo species include the pichi (*Zaedyus pichiy*), a common resident of Argentine Patagonia, and the larger hairy armadillo (*Chaetophractus villosus*), which ranges far into southern Chile.

NATURAL HISTORY

Armadillos are stout brownish animals with strong curved claws and simple peglike teeth lacking enamel. The size of armadillos varies considerably. Whereas the common nine-banded

Nine-banded armadillo (Dasypus novemcinctus). Appel Color Photography

armadillo in the United States measures about 76 cm (30 inches) long, including the tail, the pink fairy armadillo, or lesser pichiciego (*Chlamyphorus truncatus*), of central Argentina, is only about 16 cm (6 inches). In contrast, the endangered giant armadillo (*Priodontes maximus*) can be 1.5 metres (5 feet) long and weigh 30 kg (66 pounds). It lives in the Amazon Basin and adjacent grasslands.

Armadillos live alone, in pairs, or in small groups. Emerging from their burrows primarily at night, these efficient diggers use their keen sense of smell to locate food. They feed on termites and other insects, along with vegetation, small animals, and insect larvae associated with carrion. Armadillos spend the daylight hours in burrows that can be 6 metres (20 feet) long, extend 1.5 metres (5 feet) under the ground, and have up to 12 entrances. Each species digs burrows to accommodate its size and shape; other animals also use them for shelter. Because of their burrowing habits, armadillos are considered pests in many regions. Armadillo meat is eaten in various parts of South America. The common nine-banded armadillo is used in leprosy research because it is naturally susceptible to the disease and because the microbe that causes leprosy does not grow in laboratory culture media.

Armadillos are timid. When threatened, they retreat to their burrows or, if caught in the open, draw in their feet so that their armour touches the ground. Three-banded armadillos (*Tolypeutes*) are able to roll into a solid ball as a means of protecting their vulnerable underparts. Once inside a burrow, some species flex their back plates and wedge themselves in so firmly that they are virtually impossible to pull out. The pink fairy armadillo uses a different strategy. As its scientific name, *C. truncatus*, suggests, the fairy armadillo is truncated; the rear of the carapace is vertical, and the animal uses it as a flat plate to plug the entrance of its burrow. Armadillos also may run away, burrow, or claw at attackers. The nine-banded armadillo leaps vertically when startled. If captured, it reacts by "playing dead," either stiffening or relaxing but in either case remaining perfectly still. If this does not result in release, the captive armadillo begins kicking vigorously. When it encounters a body of water, *D. novemcinctus* has two options. Since its carapace is so dense that the animal cannot float, the first option is to continue walking through the water while holding its breath. Alternatively, the animal can gulp enough air into its digestive system to make itself buoyant and swim away.

Several kinds of sounds are reported to be made by fleeing or otherwise agitated armadillos. The peludos, or hairy armadillos (three species of genus *Chaetophractus*), make snarling sounds. The mulita (*D. hybridus*) repeatedly utters a guttural monosyllabic sound similar to the rapid fluttering of a human tongue.

Litter size varies from 1 to 12. The common nine-banded armadillo bears young as sets of identical quadruplets that develop in the uterus from a single fertilized egg—a phenomenon called polyembryony. The gestation period is four months in this species, but that time does not include a variable delay period of up to several months between the fertilization of the egg and its implantation in the wall of the uterus. Young are born with soft, leathery skin and can walk within a few hours after birth. The life span of this species is 12–15 years.

PALEONTOLOGY

The 20 armadillo species belong to eight genera, which together constitute the family Dasypodidae. Dasypodidae is the only family in the mammalian order Cingulata of the magnorder Xenarthra. Scaly anteaters appear similar to armadillos, as they are also armoured mammals; however, they are not found in the New World and belong to a different mammalian order (Pholidota).

Extinct relatives of today's armadillos included a 2-metre (6.6-foot), 230-kg (500-pound) beast that roamed Florida as recently as 10,000 years ago. It is not certain whether pre-Columbian humans contributed to this armadillo's extinction. A nearly complete skeleton of an even larger species, dating from the Pleistocene Epoch (2.6 million to 11,700 years ago), was found in Texas. This creature belonged to an extinct subfamily of armadillos and was nearly the size of a rhinoceros. The extinct glyptodonts were prehistoric and often massive armadillos with a single unjointed carapace.

SLOTHS

Sloths (suborder Phyllophaga) are tree-dwelling mammals noted for their slowness of movement. All five living species are limited to the lowland tropical forests of South and Central America, where they can be found high in the forest canopy sunning, resting, or feeding on leaves. Although two-toed sloths (family Megalonychidae) are capable of climbing and positioning themselves vertically, they spend almost all of their time hanging horizontally, using their large hooklike extremities to move along branches and vines. Three-toed sloths (family Bradypodidae) move in the same way but often sit in the forks of trees rather than hanging from branches.

Sloths have long legs, stumpy tails, and rounded heads with inconspicuous ears. Although they possess colour vision, sloths' eyesight and hearing are not very acute; orientation is mainly by touch. The limbs are adapted for suspending the body rather than supporting it. As a result, sloths are completely helpless on the ground unless there is something to grasp. Even then, they are able only to drag themselves along with their claws. They are surprisingly good swimmers. Generally nocturnal, sloths are solitary and are aggressive toward others of the same sex.

Sloths have large multichambered stomachs and an ability to tolerate strong chemicals from the foliage they eat. The leafy food is digested slowly; a fermenting meal may take up to a week to process. The stomach is constantly filled, its contents making up about 30 percent of the sloth's weight. Sloths descend to the ground at approximately six-day intervals to urinate and defecate. Physiologically, sloths are hetcrothermic—that is, they have imperfect control over their body temperature. Normally ranging between 25 and 35 °C (77 and 95 °F), body temperature may drop to as low as 20 °C (68 °F). At this temperature the animals become torpid. Although heterothermicity makes sloths very sensitive to temperature change, they have thick skin and are able to withstand severe injuries.

All sloths were formerly classified in the same family (Bradypodidae), but two-toed sloths have been found to be so different from three-toed sloths that they are now classified in a separate family (Megalonychidae).

Three-Toed Sloths

The three-toed sloth (family Bradypodidae) is also called the *ai* in Latin America owing to the high-pitched cry it produces when agitated. All three species belong to the same genus, *Bradypus*, and the coloration of their short facial hair bestows them with a perpetually smiling expression. The brown-throated three-toed sloth (*B. variegatus*) occurs in Central and South America from Honduras to northern Argentina; the pale-throated three-toed sloth

(*B. tridactylus*) is found in northern South America; the maned sloth (*B. torquatus*) is restricted to the small Atlantic forest of southeastern Brazil.

Although most mammals have seven neck vertebrae, three-toed sloths have eight or nine, which permits them to turn their heads through a 270° arc. The teeth are simple pegs, and the upper front pair are smaller than the others; incisor and true canine teeth are lacking. Adults weigh only about 4 kg (8.8 pounds). The head and body length of three-toed sloths averages 58 cm (23 inches), and the tail is short, round, and movable. The forelimbs are 50 percent longer than the hind limbs; all four feet have three long, curved sharp claws. Sloths' coloration makes them difficult to spot, even though they are very common in some areas. The outer layer of shaggy long hair is pale brown to gray and covers a short, dense coat of black-and-white underfur. The outer hairs have many cracks, perhaps caused by the algae living there. The algae give the animals a greenish tinge, especially during the rainy season. Sexes look alike in the maned sloth, but in the other species males have a large patch (speculum) in the middle of the back that lacks overhair, thus revealing the black dorsal stripe and bordering white underfur, which is sometimes stained yellow to orange. The maned sloth gets its name from the long black hair on the back of its head and neck.

Three-toed sloths, although mainly nocturnal, may be active day or night but spend only about 10 percent of their time moving at all. They sleep either perched in the fork of a tree or hanging from a branch, with all four feet bunched together and the head tucked in on the chest. In this posture the sloth resembles a clump of dead leaves, so inconspicuous that it was once thought these animals ate only the leaves of cecropia trees because in other trees it went undetected. Research has since shown that they eat the foliage of a wide variety of other trees and vines.

Locating food by touch and smell, the sloth feeds by hooking a branch with its claws and pulling it to its mouth. Sloths' slow movements and mainly nocturnal habits generally do not attract the attention of predators such as jaguars and harpy eagles. Normally, three-toed sloths are silent and docile, but if disturbed they can strike out furiously with the sharp foreclaws.

Reproduction is seasonal in the brown- and pale-throated species; the maned sloth may breed throughout the year. A single young is born after less than six months' gestation. Newborn sloths cling to the mother's abdomen and remain with the mother until at least five months of age. Three-toed sloths are so difficult to maintain in captivity that little is known about their breeding behaviour and other aspects of their life history.

A MOVING HABITAT: COMMUNITY ECOLOGY OF THE SLOTH

About once a week the three-toed sloth of Central and South America (*Bradypus variegatus*) descends from the trees, where it lives among the branches. For this slow-moving mammal, the journey is a dangerous and laborious undertaking, but it is one of great importance to members of the community among and aboard the sloth. Once the sloth has reached the ground, often some 30 metres (100 feet) beneath its usual perch, it digs a pit at the base of the trunk with its stubby tail. There it urinates and defecates small, hard pellets and then covers the pit with leaf litter. This process takes about 30 minutes, during which time the sloth is extremely vulnerable to predators. Although sloths are often seen in cecropia trees and may feed in 15 to 40 neighbouring trees over the course of a few months, they tend to spend most of their time in one particular "modal" tree. Up to half of the nutrients consumed by the sloth may be returned to the modal tree via the sloth's

Three-toed sloth (Bradypus tridactylus). Des Bartlett/Bruce Coleman Ltd.

buried feces. Were the feces scattered from the top of the tree, the modal tree would have to share this important resource with the plants growing on it, as well as with competing plants over a wide radius on the ground.

Other creatures, too, benefit from the sloth's weekly trip to the forest floor. The sloth carries a cargo of several species of beetles, mites, and pyralid moths in its shaggy, tan fur. They leave the sloth's body only when the animal descends, laying their eggs in the sloth's dung. Possibly the larvae aid in recycling nutrients, which the tree turns into foliage and the sloth in turn takes in as food.

The sloth's body is itself a habitat. In addition to various invertebrates, the sloth's shaggy coat, or pelage, harbours two species of blue-green algae, each hair having grooves that foster algal growth. The algae give the sloth a greenish hue, making it one of few mammals with a green coat—excellent camouflage for a slow-moving tree dweller.

TWO-TOED SLOTHS

Both species of two-toed sloth (family Megalonychidae), also called *unaus*, belong to the genus *Choloepus*. Linnaeus' two-toed sloth (*C. didactylus*) lives in northern South America east of the Andes and south to the central Amazon basin. Hoffmann's two-toed sloth (*C. hoffmanni*) is found in Central and South America from Nicaragua to Peru and western Brazil. The two species can be distinguished by the colour of the fur on the throat. Hoffmann's has a conspicuously pale throat, whereas Linnaeus's is dark.

Like the three-toed sloths, two-toed sloths have a layer of thick, long grayish brown hair with algae growing in it that covers a short coat of underfur. But whereas the three-toed sloth's outer hairs are cracked transversely, those of the two-toed sloth have longitudinal grooves that harbour algae. The overhair is parted on the abdomen and hangs down over the sides of its body.

Two-toed sloths are slightly larger than three-toed sloths. The head and body are about 60–70 cm (24–27 inches) long, and adults weigh up to 8 kg (17.6 pounds). The two-clawed forelimbs are only somewhat longer than the hind limbs, which have three claws. Although most mammals have seven neck vertebrae, and three-toed sloths have eight or nine, two-toed sloths have only six or seven. Normally docile and reliant on their concealing coloration for protection, two-toed sloths, if molested, will snort and hiss, bite savagely, and slash with their sharp foreclaws.

A single young is born after almost 12 months' gestation. The offspring emerges head first and face upward as the mother hangs. As soon as the baby's front limbs are free, it grasps the abdominal hair of the mother and pulls itself to her chest. The mother sometimes assists in birth by pulling on the young. The mother then chews through the umbilical cord, and the young sloth, after its eyes and ears open, clings to the fur of the mother for about five weeks. After it leaves the mother, it reaches maturity in two to three years. In captivity, two toed-sloths have lived more than 20 years; maximum life span is thought to be over 30.

PALEONTOLOGY

All sloths were formerly included in the family Bradypodidae, but the two-toed sloths have been found to be of a different family, Megalonychidae, whose extinct relatives, the ground sloths, once ranged into areas of the North American continent as far as Alaska and southern

Canada. Different species of ground sloths varied greatly in size. Most were small, but one, the giant ground sloth (*Megatherium americanum*), was the size of an elephant; others were as tall as present-day giraffes. The period of the ground sloths' extinction coincides approximately with the end of the last Ice Age and the arrival of humans in North America.

Anteaters

There are four known species of anteaters (suborder Vermilingua). They are toothless, insect-eating mammals found in tropical savannas and forests from southern Mexico to Paraguay and northern Argentina. Anteaters are long-tailed animals with elongated skulls and tubular muzzles. The mouth opening of the muzzle is small, but the salivary glands are large and secrete sticky saliva onto a wormlike tongue, which can be as long as 60 cm (24 inches) in the giant anteater. Anteaters live alone or in pairs (usually mother and offspring) and feed mainly on ants and termites. They capture their prey by inserting their tongues into insect nests that they have torn open with the long, sharp, curved claws of their front feet; the claws are also used for defense. Giant anteaters and the smaller tamanduas (described on page 217) use their hind legs and tail as a tripod when threatened, which thus frees the front limbs to slash at attackers.

The Giant Anteaters

The giant anteater (*Myrmecophaga tridactyla*), sometimes called the ant bear, is the largest member of the anteater family and is best known in the tropical grasslands (Llanos) of Venezuela, where it is still common. It was once found in the lowland forests of Central America and still lives in the Amazon basin southward to the grasslands of Paraguay and Argentina. Gray with a diagonal white-bordered black stripe on each shoulder, the giant anteater attains a length of about 1.8 metres (6 feet), including the long bushy tail, and weighs up to 40 kg (88 pounds). This ground dweller is mainly diurnal, but in areas near human settlement it is most active at night.

Using its keen sense of smell to track ants, the giant anteater walks with a shuffle, bearing its weight on the sides and knuckles of its forefeet. When harried, it is capable of a clumsy gallop. The giant anteater is also a good swimmer. It does not seem to use dens or other resting places on a permanent basis but chooses instead a secluded spot where it can curl up to rest, with its huge tail covering both its head and its body. Females bear a single offspring after a gestation period of about 190 days. With the exception of size, a young anteater looks identical to an adult, and from two or three weeks following birth until it is about a year old it rides on its mother's back as she travels. The home ranges of individual anteaters living in the Llanos overlap and can cover more than 2,500 hectares (6,000 acres). The giant anteater is the longest-lived anteater; one in captivity reportedly survived 25 years.

giant anteater
(*Myrmecophaga tridactyla*)

30 cm
12 inches

Encyclopædia Britannica, Inc.

PANGOLINS

Pangolins, which are also called scaly anteaters, are armoured placental mammals of the order Pholidota. Pangolin, from the Malayan meaning "rolling over," refers to this animal's habit of curling into a ball when threatened. About eight species of pangolins, usually considered to be of the genus *Manis,* family Manidae, are found in tropical Asia and Africa. Pangolins are 30 to 90 cm (1 to 3 feet) long exclusive of the tail and weigh from 5 to 27 kg (10 to 60 pounds). Except for the sides of the face and underside of the body, they are covered with overlapping brownish scales composed of cemented hairs. The head is short and conical, with small, thickly lidded eyes and a long, toothless muzzle; the tongue is wormlike and extensile, up to 25 cm (10 inches) in length. The legs are short, and the five-toed feet have sharp claws. The tail, about as long as the body, is prehensile, and, with the hind legs, it forms a tripod for support.

Some pangolins, such as the African black-bellied pangolin (*Manis longicaudata*) and the Chinese pangolin (*M. pentadactyla*), are almost entirely arboreal; others, such as the giant pangolin (*M. gigantea*) of Africa, are terrestrial. All are nocturnal and able to swim a little. Terrestrial forms live in burrows. Pangolins feed mainly on termites but also eat ants and other insects. They locate prey by smell and use the forefeet to rip open nests.

Their means of defense are the emission of an odorous secretion from large anal glands and the ploy of rolling up, presenting erected scales to the enemy. Pangolins are timid and live alone or in pairs. Apparently usually one young is born at a time, soft-scaled at birth and carried on the female's back for some time. Life span is about 12 years.

Pangolins were once grouped with anteaters, sloths, and armadillos, mainly because of superficial likenesses to South American anteaters. Pangolins differ from xenarthrans, however, in many fundamental anatomic characteristics, and thus are found beyond the geographic range of true xenarthrans.

The earliest fossil Pholidota are bones indistinguishable from those of the African giant pangolin, found in a cave in India and dating to the Pleistocene Epoch (2,600,000 to 11,700 years ago).

THE TAMANDUAS

Unlike the giant anteater, the lesser anteater, or tamandua (genus *Tamandua*), is arboreal as well as terrestrial. The two tamandua species are similar in size—about 1.2 metres (4 feet) long, including the almost-hairless prehensile tail, which is used for climbing. They are often tan with a blackish "vest" around the shoulders and on the body, but some are entirely tan or entirely black. Tamanduas have shorter fur and proportionately shorter muzzles than giant anteaters.

The lesser anteater (Tamandua tetradactyla) *lives primarily in trees and feeds during the night. To ward off predators, the tamandua may release a very unpleasant odour from a gland at the base of its tail.* Shutterstock.com

The tamandua, meaning "catcher of ants" in the Tupí language of eastern Brazil, eats both termites and ants and often uses the same pathway repeatedly in search of food. Although many species of ants are eaten by tamanduas, they are selective, eating relatively few ants of any given colony and avoiding those with painful stings or bites, such as army ants (genus *Eciton*). Tamandua dens can be found in hollow trees and logs or in the ground, and individual home ranges cover about 75 hectares (185 acres). The northern tamandua (*T. mexicana*) is found from eastern Mexico to northwestern South America; the southern tamandua (*T. tetradactyla*) is found from the island of Trinidad southward to northern Argentina.

The Silky Anteaters

Also known as the two-toed, pygmy, or dwarf anteater, the silky anteater (*Cyclopes didactylus*) is the smallest and least-known member of the family. The silky anteater is found from southern Mexico southward to Bolivia and Brazil. It is not rare but is difficult to spot because it is nocturnal and lives high in the trees. It is also exquisitely camouflaged, its silky yellowish coat matching both the colour and the texture of fibrous seed masses produced by the silk-cotton tree. During the day the silky anteater rests amid clumps of tropical vines.

Silky anteaters seldom exceed 300 grams (11 ounces). The animal's maximum overall length is about 44 cm (17 inches). About one-half of that length is the furred prehensile tail. There are two clawed toes on each forefoot. (The forefoot of the tamandua has four clawed toes, whereas that of the giant anteater has three prominent clawed toes flanked by two small toes.) The silky anteater has large eyes that allow foraging at night. The feet are equipped with heel pads that can be opposed against the claws, enabling the animal to grip small branches as it

Silky anteater (Cyclopes didactylus) *extending its long, narrow tongue, which it uses to capture and ingest prey.* Gunter Ziesler/Bruce Coleman Ltd.

travels the forest canopy along lianas (climbing plants) and other vines. Males live in territories of 5–10 hectares (12–25 acres) that overlap with those of several females.

CLASSIFICATION

The giant anteater and tamanduas constitute the family Myrmecophagidae, which means "ant-eating" in Latin, whereas the silky anteater is classified in a family of its own, Cyclopedidae. Together the two families make up the anteater suborder, Vermilingua. A number of animals unrelated to the myrmecophagids are also called anteaters. The banded anteater, for example, is a marsupial. The scaly anteater was formerly grouped with xenarthrans in an order called Edentata, but it has since been assigned to its own separate order. The short-beaked echidna is often called a spiny anteater, but this animal is even more distantly related. The African aardvark also belongs to a different mammalian order, yet, like the anteater, it has a tubular muzzle for eating ants and is sometimes called an antbear.

CONCLUSION

In terms of species, rodents and bats together account for over half of the world's mammals, and both groups have representatives throughout the world. Rodents, the family Muridae in particular, have been fantastically successful. Some rodent species have easily adapted to the changes in land use brought about by human activity and often co-occur with humans in urban areas. Some species are well-known pests.

Although bats do not thrive in human-dominated landscapes, they are also very diverse. Most bat species occur in the tropics, preferring the warmer regions of the world. Ecologically, they are important agents of pollination and insect control. Some species, such as the Mexican free-tailed bat (*Tadarida brasiliensis mexicana*), are very abundant.

In stark contrast to the diversity of rodents and bats, modern xenarthrans are made up of only 29 living species. In addition, all true members of this group occur in the New World, mainly in Latin America. Although most xenarthrans are insectivores, they do not have the ecological impact of rodents or bats. Within their home range, however, some xenarthrans, such as the sloths, are important parts of the ecosystems they inhabit.

GLOSSARY

alluvium Clay, silt, sand, gravel, or similar material deposited by running water.

appurtenance Appendage.

arboreal Inhabiting or frequenting trees.

arthropod Any of a phylum (Arthropoda) of invertebrate animals (as insects, arachnids, and crustaceans) that have a segmented body and jointed appendages.

artiodactyl Any of an order (Artiodactyla) of ungulates (as the camel or pig) with an even number of functional toes on each foot.

biped A two-footed animal.

boreal Of, relating to, or located in northern regions.

brackish Of, relating to a volume of mixed fresh and salt water.

butte An isolated hill or mountain with steep or precipitous sides usually having a smaller summit area than a mesa.

cached Hidden; stored.

cambium In plants, a layer of actively dividing cells between xylem (fluid-conducting) and phloem (food-conducting) tissues that is responsible for the secondary growth of stems and roots, resulting in an increase in thickness.

carapace A bony or horny case or shield covering the back or part of the back of an animal (as a turtle, crab, or armadillo).

carrion The dead and rotting flesh of an animal.

cartilaginous Composed of, relating to, or resembling cartilage.

cassava An edible tropical American plant (*Manihot esculenta*) with large, tuberous, starchy roots.

castor A bitter strong-smelling creamy orange-brown substance that consists of the dried perineal glands of the beaver and their secretion and is used by perfumers as a fixative and by professional trappers to scent bait. Also called *castoreum*.

cecropia Several species of tropical tree of the family Cecropiaceae common to the understory layer of disturbed forest habitats of Central and South America. It is easily recognized by its thin, white-ringed trunk and umbrella-like arrangement of large leaves at the branch tips.

chaparral A dense impenetrable thicket of shrubs or dwarf trees.

conifer Any of an order (Coniferales) of mostly evergreen trees and shrubs having usually needle-shaped or scale-like leaves and including forms (as pines) with true cones and others (as yews) with fruit.

corral A pen or enclosure for confining or capturing livestock.

deciduous Falling off or shedding at the end of the growing period.

degenerative Of or relating to a progressive degeneration. Degeneration, in turn, is a secondary simplification of a part or organism in the course of generations often to the extent of loss of function or complete disappearance of constituent structures .

dentine A material composed of calcium carbonate similar to but harder and denser than bone that composes the principal mass of a tooth.

dermestid Any member of about 700 species (family Dermestidae) of widely distributed beetles that are household pests.

diastema A space between teeth in a jaw.

dike An artificial watercourse (as for drainage).

disjunct Non-contiguous; now used almost entirely of distributions (as of statistical or natural populations).

diurnal Active chiefly in the daytime.

Doppler shift Also known as the Doppler effect, a change in frequency of an electromagnetic radiation caused by the motions of the atoms, molecules, or nuclei in the line of sight.

extant Currently existing.

fallow Cultivated land that is allowed to lie idle during the growing season.

folivorous An herbivorous animal or organism that specializes in eating leaves, such as the sloth.

forb An herb other than grass.

fencerow The land occupied by a fence including the uncultivated area on each side.

genera Plural form of genus.

glyptodont An extinct armour-covered mammal of the genus *Glyptodon*.

grizzled Gray.

hantavirus Any member of a genus of viruses (Hantavirus) of the family Bunyaviridae that cause acute respiratory illnesses in humans.

heath An extensive area of rather level open uncultivated land usually with poor coarse soil.

hectare Unit of area in the metric system equal to 100 acres, or 10,000 square metres, and the equivalent of 2.471 acres in the British Imperial System and the United States Customary measure.

hedgerow A row of shrubs or trees enclosing or separating fields.

hispid Rough or covered with bristles, stiff hairs, or minute spines.

husbandry The scientific control and management of a branch of farming and especially of domestic animals.

leptospirosis Any of several diseases of humans and domestic animals that are caused by infection with leptospires, a kind of bacteria.

magnorder A level in traditional taxonomy (traditional taxonomy being that based on observable similarities, such as shape, as opposed to DNA) that exists between class and order.

mangrove Any tropical tree or shrub of the genus Rhizophora growing in marshes or tidal shores, noted for their interlacing above-ground roots.

marsupial A group of mammals that possess a pouch for carrying the young.

masseter A large muscle that raises the lower jaw and assists in chewing.

melanistic Affected with or characterized by melanism, an unusual development of black or nearly black colour in the skin or in the plumage or pelage occurring either as a characteristic of a variety or as an individual variation especially in mammals and birds.

midden An accumulation of refuse about a dwelling place: a refuse heap.

monophyletic Developed from a single common ancestral form.

montane A mountainous region composed of coniferous trees below the tree line.

morphology The form and structure of an organism or any of its parts.

murine typhus A mild disease that is marked especially by fever, headache, and rash, is caused by a rickettsia (*Rickettsia typhi* syn. *R. mooseri*), is widespread in nature in rodents, and is transmitted to humans by a flea.

nicitating membrane A thin membrane found in many animals at the inner angle or beneath the lower lid of the eye and capable of extending across the eyeball.

olfactory Of or relating to the sense of smell.

omnivorous Feeding on both animal and vegetable substances.

pika Small short-legged and virtually tailless egg-shaped mammal found in the mountains of western North America and much of Asia.

polymorphic The quality or state of existing in or assuming different forms.

predation A mode of life in which food is primarily obtained by the killing and consuming of animals.

prehensile Adapted for seizing or grasping, especially by wrapping around, as a monkey's tail.

pyralid moth Any of a group of moths in the order Lepidoptera, most members of which have long, narrow forewings, broader hindwings, and a wingspan of 18 to 35 mm (0.75 to 1.5 inches).

relict A surviving species of an otherwise extinct group of organisms.

rhizome A horizontal, underground plant stem capable of producing the shoot and root systems of a new plant.

riverine Situated along the banks of a river.

schistosomiasis A severe disease of humans caused by small, parasitic flatworms and that is marked especially by blood loss and tissue damage.

sedge family Family Cyperaceae, one of the 10 largest families of flowering plants, composed of about 5,000 species of grass-like herbs that inhabit wet regions worldwide.

spermatogenesis The origin and development of the sperm cells within the male reproductive organs, the testes.

sphagnum Peat moss.

suffuse To fill; spread through or over, as with colour.

tactile Having the sense of touch.

taxonomy Classification; especially: orderly classification of plants and animals according to their presumed natural relationships. Taxon (plural *taxa*) is the name applied to any taxonomic group.

torpor A state of lowered physiological activity typically characterized by reduced metabolism, heart rate, respiration, and body temperature that occurs in varying degrees especially in hibernating animals.

trypanosomiasis An infectious disease in both humans and animals spread by certain bloodsucking insects.

tubercle A small knobby prominence especially on a plant or animal: nodule.

tularemia Acute infectious disease resembling plague, but much less severe. It is generally transmitted by the bites of insects or ticks. The disease is primarily one of animals; human infections are incidental.

tussock A compact tuft especially of grass or sedge; *also*: an area of raised solid ground in a marsh or bog that is bound together by roots of low vegetation.

variegate To diversify especially in external appearance (as with different colours).

vector An organism (as an insect) that transmits disease.

BIBLIOGRAPHY

RODENTS

The order Rodentia is treated most extensively within larger works about mammals, but the following sources cover rodents exclusively.

David Alderton and Bruce Tanner, *Rodents of the World* (1996, reissued 1999), provides a concise, well-illustrated description of rodents and also includes distribution maps. Eileen A. Lacey, James L. Patton, and Guy N. Cameron, (eds.), *Life Underground: The Biology of Subterranean Rodents* (2000), a worldwide survey that compares and contrasts evolutionary, anatomic, and other biological similarities between burrowing species. J.R. Ellerman, *The Families and Genera of Living Rodents*, 2 vol. (1940–41, reprinted 2 vol. in 1, 1966), is a scientific catalog of living rodents that is considered a classic; Robert Hendrickson, *More Cunning than Man: A Social History of Rats and Man* (1983, reissued 1999), describes a variety of roles, both positive and negative, that rats have played in their relationship with humans.

Edited volumes covering all mammals but containing separate rodent chapters or species accounts written by specialists include Don E. Wilson and Sue Ruff (eds.), *The Smithsonian Book of North American Mammals* (1999); and Ronald Strahan (ed.), *Mammals of Australia*, rev. ed. (1995, reissued 1998).

Additional works that include substantial sections on rodents are Ronald M. Nowak, *Walker's Mammals of the World*, 6th ed., 2 vol. (1999); David Macdonald (ed.), *The Encyclopedia of Mammals* (1984, reprinted 1999); John

O. Whitaker, Jr., and William J. Hamilton, Jr., *Mammals of the Eastern United States*, 3rd ed. (1998); M.G.L. Mills and Lex Hes (compilers), *The Complete Book of Southern African Mammals* (1997); G.B. Corbet and J.E. Hill, *The Mammals of the Indomalayan Region* (1992); and Timothy Flannery, *Mammals of New Guinea*, rev. and updated ed. (1995), and *Mammals of the South-West Pacific & Moluccan Islands* (1995).

Field guides containing sections on rodents include John O. Whitaker, Jr., *National Audubon Society Field Guide to North American Mammals*, 2nd ed. (1996, reissued 1998); Louise H. Emmons and François Feer, *Neotropical Rainforest Mammals: A Field Guide*, 2nd ed. (1997); Jonathan Kingdon, *The Kingdon Field Guide to African Mammals* (1997); and Junaidi Payne, Charles M. Francis, and Karen Phillipps, *A Field Guide to the Mammals of Borneo* (1985).

Taxonomy is the primary focus of Malcolm C. McKenna and Susan K. Bell, *Classification of Mammals Above the Species Level* (1997), which formally classifies living and fossil mammals. Don E. Wilson and DeeAnn M. Reeder (eds.), *Mammal Species of the World: A Taxonomic and Geographic Reference*, 2nd ed. (1993), briefly lists the synonyms, distributions, and original scientific publications for each of the world's mammalian species.

BATS

M. Brock Fenton, *Bats*, rev. ed. (2005), a coffee-table book, is nicely illustrated and full of useful information. Klaus Richarz and Alfred Limbrunner, *The World of Bats* (1993), has good information on bat biology and excellent colour photographs.

N.B. Simmons, "Order Chiroptera," in Don E. Wilson and DeeAnn M. Reeder (eds.), *Mammal Species of the World*, 3rd ed. (2005), offers a complete list of bat species of the world, with information on their taxonomy and geographic distribution.

Don E. Wilson and Sue Ruff (eds.), *The Smithsonian Book of North American Mammals* (1999), contains a summary of what is known about each species of bat in North America. Fiona A. Reid, *A Field Guide to the Mammals of Central America and Southeast Mexico* (1997), includes detailed accounts of each species of bat in this biologically diverse region. Louise H. Emmons, *Neotropical Rainforest Mammals*, 2nd ed. (1999), provides similar coverage for most South American forms. Hugh H. Genoways et al., *Bats of Jamaica* (2005), pulls together all of the disparate natural history information about the species of bats found on this large Caribbean island.

John D. Altringham, *British Bats* (2003), has detailed species accounts, plus hints on practical projects, equipment, conservation and identification, and the law. Wilfried Schober and Eckard Grimmberger, *The Bats of Europe & North America*, trans. by William Charlton (1997), takes an in-depth look at European bat biology, accompanied by lavish illustrations of most species. Jonathan Kingdon, *The Kingdon Field Guide to African Mammals* (1997, reissued 2003), provides some identification aids to common species of African bats. Gus Mills and Lex Hes, *The Complete Book of Southern African Mammals* (1997), documents information on all bat species found in southern Africa.

Sue Churchill, *Australian Bats* (1998), is a comprehensive identification guide to the many species of bats found in Australia. Tim Flannery, *Mammals of New Guinea*, rev. and updated ed. (1995), provides information on all known bat species from New Guinea, in a beautifully illustrated format; his *Mammals of the South-west Pacific & Moluccan Islands* (1995), extends that coverage to surrounding island areas. G.B. Corbet and J.E. Hill, *The Mammals of the Indomalayan Region: A Systematic Review* (1992), covers all species of bats in Southeast Asia. Paul J.J. Bates and David L. Harrison, *Bats of the Indian Subcontinent* (1997), is an excellent compilation of knowledge about bats of India and surrounding regions.

John D. Altringham, *Bats: Biology and Behaviour* (1996, reissued 1999), with thorough coverage of bat biology, is aimed at students but is accessible to the general public as well. Sue Ruff and Don E. Wilson, *Bats* (2001), is a well-illustrated summary of bat biology that is aimed at the primary-school level. James S. Findley, *Bats: A Community Perspective*, new ed. (1994), is a comprehensive look at the community structure of bats.

Jeannette A. Thomas, Cynthia F. Moss, and Marianne Vater (eds.), *Echolocation in Bats and Dolphins* (2004), compares what is known about echolocation in both of these groups. L. van der Pijl, *Principles of Dispersal in Higher Plants*, 3rd rev. and expanded ed. (1982), covers the role of bats in dispersal of seeds.

XENARTHRANS

Alfred L. Gardner, "Order Xenarthra," in Don E. Wilson and DeeAnn M. Reeder (eds.), *Mammal Species of the World: A Taxonomic and Geographic Reference* (1993), pp. 63–68, provides lists of the families, genera, and species of the Xenarthra; the author is a wildlife biologist and curator of mammals at the Smithsonian's National Museum of Natural History. Gerald G. Montgomery (ed.), *The Evolution and Ecology of Armadillos, Sloths, and Vermilinguas* (1985), compiles 43 well-illustrated scholarly reports on all aspects of xenarthran biology, including pathology and parasitology.

INDEX

viscachas, 24, 119, 127, 139–142
  mountain, 140–141, 142
  plains, 141–142
voles, 5, 53, 63, 76–79, 95, 137

W

Wagner's mustached bat, 165
water rats, 6, 41–43
  African, 42, 43
  earless, 42–43
  golden-bellied, 42
woodchucks, 94, 116–118
woodland voles, 76, 77–79
wood mice, 50, 61–63, 74
  Japanese, 62

long-tailed field mice, 62
striped field mice, 62
woodrats, 31–34

X

xenarthrans, 202–220
  paleontology of, 204

Y

yellow-winged bats, 157

Z

zokors, 5, 151–152